AF248574

"*Two Masters* is a masterful example of Southern regional writing at its best."

Scott Fosdick
Baltimore News American

"One brief play that ... managed to overshadow all other contenders. This was *The Rain of Terror*."

Mel Gussow
The New York Times

" ... Manley has crafted a small but well-made play expertly intertwining the multiple threads of plot, character, and theme."

Hillary DeVries
The Christian Science Monitor

PLAYS BY
Frank Manley

TWO MASTERS

PRIOR ENGAGEMENTS

SUSAN
HUNTER
Publishing

Atlanta, Georgia

Manley, Frank.
    [Two masters]
    Two masters: Prior engagements: plays / Frank Manley.
    p. cm.
    ISBN 0-932419-14-3:
    I. Manley, Frank. Prior engagements. 1987. II. Title.
PS3563.A517T9 1987   87-24619
812' .54–dc19   CIP

Published by Susan Hunter Publishing, Atlanta, Georgia
Manufactured in the United States of America
5 4 3 2 1
Publisher: Susan Hunter
Editor: Phyllis Mueller

Photo credits:

Front cover: David S. Talbott, courtesy of
            Actors Theatre of Louisville

The Rain of Terror: David S. Talbott, courtesy of
            Actors Theatre of Louisville

An Errand of Mercy: David S. Talbott, courtesy of
            Actors Theatre of Louisville

The Baptism of Water: Jennifer Girard, courtesy of
            Victory Gardens Theatre

Chickamauga: courtesy of Theater Emory

The Call of Nature: Jennifer Girard, courtesy of
            Victory Gardens Theatre

Back cover photo: Billy Howard

CONTENTS

TWO MASTERS

The Rain of Terror   3
An Errand of Mercy   37

PRIOR ENGAGEMENTS

The Baptism of Water   73
Chickamauga   97
The Call of Nature   131

*For Mary Catherine, Michael,
David, and Peter*

TWO MASTERS

Two Masters was first produced by Theater Emory, Emory University, in the fall of 1984, after having received a workshop production sponsored by Theater Emory in the Atlanta New Play Project in June 1984. It was directed by James W. Flannery with Sandra Deer serving as dramaturg. The set and lighting were designed by Randy Fullerton. The production manager was Robert Schultz, and the cast consisted of Suzi Bass, Pat Hurley, and Brenda Bynum.

It was later performed in March 1985 at Actors Theatre, Louisville, Kentucky, as part of the Ninth Annual Humana Festival of New American Plays, where it was named co-winner of the Great American New Play Contest. It was directed by Jackson Phippin, and the cast consisted of Kathy Bates, Andy Backer, Adele O'Brien, and Beth Dixon. The stage manager was Anne King, assisted by Larry Varvel. The set was designed by Paul Owen and the costumes by Marcia Dixcy.

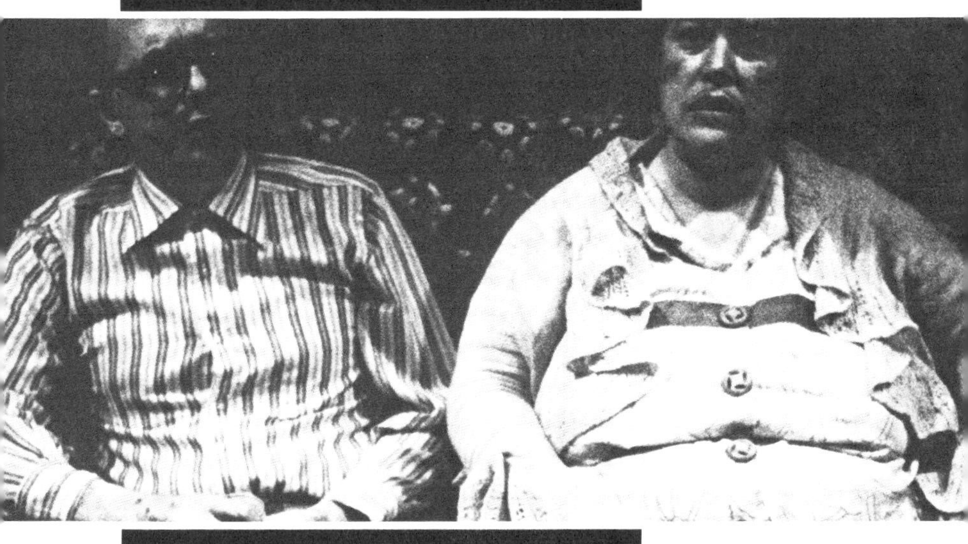

The Rain of Terror

CAST OF CHARACTERS

OLETTA CREWS, an old woman
JAMES TERRY CREWS, her husband

Darkness.

The sound of rain and in it, distant music.

A point of light appears and grows in intensity to reveal an old man and an old woman sitting side by side on a small sofa or love seat. The sofa is located as close to the front of the stage as possible so as to allow the actors to lean forward and speak confidentially to the members of the audience, catching their eye and addressing them directly. The audience functions as something like the third character in the play. Its role is to sit in judgment on what turns out to be a mutilated ritual of expiation.

The old man and woman are dressed in ordinary work clothes — the man in khaki trousers and six-inch work boots; the woman in a print dress — a bold floral pattern like slashes. She wears no shoes. The man dips snuff or chews tobacco. He uses a spit can. The woman nurses a coke and smokes cigarettes. The remainder of the stage is bare. The only reality is the old man and the old woman and the sofa on which they sit. The feeling is that of a cave or a nest — the secret bestial place.

OLETTA CREWS, *as in a public announcement:* My name is Oletta Crews. *Pauses.* This is James Terry Crews, my husband — *indicating the old man beside her. James Terry Crews gestures silently toward the audience acknowledging himself.*

OLETTA CREWS: Don't act like an idiot. *James Terry Crews drops his hand.* Just sit there. *She turns to face the audience again.* This is James Terry Crews, my husband — *in a powerful voice, lifted like a singer from out of her diaphragm.* He's retired. *She pauses. Significantly:* We're both retired. Him from work and me from housework. I got a bad heart, and I'm stout besides. You can see that. Doctor says I'm hundreds of pounds overweight, shortening my life with every bite of food I take. But what if I don't? You think that'd help? *She leans forward and speaks confidentially:* There's more dies of hunger than does of the other. *She leans back and gestures toward her husband again.* He does what he needs to.

James Terry Crews sits beside her and stares at the audience as though afraid.

Silence.

OLETTA CREWS: Listen to me. *James Terry Crews starts to rise, but she holds out a hand to restrain him.* Sit there. *She turns to the audience:* Listen. I live here alone all by myself, a poor old woman except for him — *gesturing toward James Terry Crews sitting beside her.* He lives here too. Both together. *She pauses.* This is a trailer, you notice that?

JAMES TERRY CREWS, *correcting her:* Mobile home.

OLETTA CREWS, *turning toward him, suddenly angry:* Same damn thing. I told you that. Pay attention.

James Terry Crews ignores her and appeals directly to the audience.

JAMES TERRY CREWS: Trailer's something you

trail. That's what it means, trailer. You hitch it on the back of a car and hit the trail.

OLETTA CREWS, *shouting*: And mobile home's mobile. That means it moves. *It seems like an argument they have had before, the lines already memorized, the positions not only known, but entrenched and fortified.*

JAMES TERRY CREWS: Tell them about the rain of terror.

OLETTA CREWS, *savoring the words*: The rain of terror. *She turns to James Terry Crews*: They don't want to hear about mobile homes. They want to hear about the rain of terror. *She bugs her eyes as she says the rain of terror. The effect is not comic. Her eyes are filled with something other than fear*: It was at night.

JAMES TERRY CREWS: Two nights ago. *He speaks to the audience as though to himself. He sounds incredulous.*

OLETTA CREWS, *beginning again*: It was two nights ago, and it was dark. James Terry was already home soaking wet from the weeds where he'd been and changed his clothes already to dry them. He was picking aluminum cans. I'm too stout to get out and help, or else I'd be there driving the truck, but I can't even drive no more. It's bad on my heart, and the pedals are too close anyway. They're all underfoot. *She leans forward and speaks confidentially to the audience*: It's hell to be old. If I was you, I'd die before I get there, *laughing silently, baring her gums.*

JAMES TERRY CREWS, *announcing to the audience*: I used to be a house painter. Twenty-eight years and every day sober on the job.

OLETTA CREWS, *shouting*: They don't want to hear

that. You're retired. *Turning back to the audience*: He sells aluminum cans. That's what he does now. They got a yard in town buys them. Beer cans and such as that.

JAMES TERRY CREWS: I didn't always do it. I used to paint with the best of them.

OLETTA CREWS: That was then. This is now. *She turns back to the audience*. I'm telling this. *She picks up where she left off*. He came in sopping wet from the rain of terror where he'd been in the weeds all day looking for beer cans and I told him what I saw on TV so he don't fall too far behind. And he was changing his socks. I can close my eyes and still see him sitting right there — *pointing* — changing his socks when I heard this knocking at the door, and I said, 'Who's that?'

JAMES TERRY CREWS: What did you think?

OLETTA CREWS: I thought, Who's that?

JAMES TERRY CREWS: Me too. I thought, Who's that.

OLETTA CREWS: I thought, Who's that knocking on the door in the dark? I knew it wasn't nobody I knew. His children gone and I don't have none, and all my kinfolks are dead before me.

JAMES TERRY CREWS: Tell them about the news.

OLETTA CREWS: I don't generally watch the news if I can help it, but this night was special. The good Lord led me to it this night. It's like I almost heard this voice said, 'Don't touch the TV. I got something on the news.' I was too tired to get up, and it said, 'Don't do it then. There's something better for you to do than get up and change the channel. I got something to show you right here on this one you're watching.' It's like I heard this voice inside me beside the still waters, leading me on in the valley of the shadow of death where I fear no evil for thou art with me. Thy rod and thy staff, they comfort me.

JAMES TERRY CREWS: And you were afraid.

OLETTA CREWS: Course I was afraid after hearing what I heard and knowing it was some kind of message delivered on TV special for me. Course I was afraid. Who wouldn't be? I knew he'd protect me, like he did. That's why I'm alive and the other one dead cause I could walk through the valley of the shadow of death and fear no evil. So the answer is, No. No, I wasn't afraid. But I was interested. When I heard how he escaped from the work camp and killed two men and it wasn't more than five miles down the road and was coming this way, I wasn't afraid, but I was interested.

JAMES TERRY CREWS: She heard the knock.

OLETTA CREWS: I heard the knock and wondered, 'Who is it?' But I already know. I said, 'It's him.'

JAMES TERRY CREWS: And I said 'Who?'

OLETTA CREWS, *shouting*: Let me tell it. You weren't even there when it happened. I'm telling it. Listen. This is how it happened. I heard that knock and I said, 'It's him,' and James Terry looked up from his sock and said 'Who do you mean?' And I said, 'The one on TV when you wasn't here and killed two men. It's him at the door,' and he put his sock on — *indicating her husband* — and said, 'What you want to do?' And I said, 'Go get it. He might have some money hid.'

JAMES TERRY CREWS: And I said, Money? What you mean money?

OLETTA CREWS: Where he hid it after he stole it. That's why they escape, to go get the money they hid. I thought he might have some, and I said, 'Let him in. He might have some money hid.' And James Terry went to the door, one shoe on and one in his hand. And it was him. *Pauses.* I was sitting right here where I always sit, and I saw him standing in the door soaking wet where it was raining outside as far as the eye could see. Looked like silver knives. And he said, 'Can I come in? I'm awful wet.' And I yelled, 'I can see you are, honey. Let him in, James Terry. Let him in to get dry.' And he came in, and I said, 'Get him a towel.' And James Terry got him a towel and sat down to put on his shoe. And I said to him, 'I know who you are.'

JAMES TERRY CREWS: She knew who he was.

OLETTA CREWS: I told him I saw his picture on TV, and I knew who he was, thanks to God, and what he was there for.

JAMES TERRY CREWS: What was that?

OLETTA CREWS: You were there. Don't ask things you already know. He was there to rob us — *to the audience.* He came here to rob us.

JAMES TERRY CREWS: Your life was in danger.

OLETTA CREWS, *surprised:* My life was in danger. As soon as I saw him, I knew I might not live. *Pauses.*

JAMES TERRY CREWS: Go on.

OLETTA CREWS: I said, 'You're Q.B. Farris, escaped from the work camp.' And he said, 'Yes ma'am. I can't fool you. I can see that.' And I said 'That's right. There's many a one better than you tried all my life, and they didn't do it, so why should you?' And he laughed. *Pauses.* He was good hearted. I can say that for him. He might have been mean, but he was good hearted. He didn't care.

JAMES TERRY CREWS: I liked him.

OLETTA CREWS: Then he said, 'You know who I am? You know what I done?' And I said, 'Some. I know the most recent.' And I told him he killed two men. And he said that was exaggerated. And I said, 'It's on TV.' And he said he didn't care. It was exaggerated. And I said, 'Don't kill me. I'm just a poor old woman. It won't help to kill me. I don't know where your money's hid.' And I saw him looking at James Terry Crews where he'd just finished putting on his shoe, and I said, 'Don't kill him either. He got to help me. I'm retired.' And he laughed like he done and said, 'What you retired from, momma?' And I said, 'Don't call me momma. I ain't your momma.' I ain't nobody's momma! And he said, 'You look like you ought to be. You got a kind face and a big bosom.' And I thought then, he's going to rape me. Been in prison with men too long.

JAMES TERRY CREWS: His name was Duke.

OLETTA CREWS: Q.B. Farris. He said his name was Duke. He said, 'Call me Duke. I don't know who Q.B. is.'

JAMES TERRY CREWS: And I said, 'What's the Q.B. stand for?' And you know what he said? He said, 'Queer Bastard.' I didn't know what to make of that.

OLETTA CREWS, *shouting*: Except he wasn't queer, or else he wouldn't have wanted to rape me.

JAMES TERRY CREWS: Unless he was both.

OLETTA CREWS: I'm telling this. We already agreed to that. *To audience.* That's the kind of person he was, full of useless jokes like that. He didn't care.

You know what he said when I said, 'Don't kill me'?
He said, 'I wouldn't kill you or him either, momma. I
got a momma of my own.' And I said, 'Well, where is
she? You say you got a momma. Where is she?'
I figured she might have the money. And he said,
'Oconee, Tennessee — in the graveyard' and looked at
me and laughed. And I said, 'You laughing because
she's dead or you laughing cause you broke her heart?'
That straightened him out. He quit laughing and said,
'Neither one. I loved my momma. She's the only one I
trust.' And I said, 'I reckon. I'd trust her too, state
she's in now.' That's when he hit me.

JAMES TERRY CREWS, *shocked*: He hit you?

OLETTA CREWS: He tried to. And then he stopped.
He looked at me and said, 'She died when I was still in
prison. I never got to go to the funeral cause it was out
of state.' Said if it'd been in the state, they'd have let
him, but she was buried in Tennessee, and that's a
whole other system. And I thought, So what? She
wouldn't know if you were there or not — chained like
a wild dog at a funeral. I told him, 'She'd have died if
you were in jail or not.' And he said it wasn't the
dying he minded. It was they wouldn't let him out.
That's what he hated. And he told me about the nine
years. He said, 'I ain't been my own man in nine years
and nine more to go.' And I thought whose fault is
that? Don't come crying on my shoulder. You should
have thought about that when you decided what you
wanted to be.

JAMES TERRY CREWS: What do you mean?

OLETTA CREWS: What do I mean? I mean a robber
— steals money and hides it somewhere. And I said,
'Your momma's house still standing? That where
you're going?' And he said, no he liked it here. And I
said, 'I don't got no money. You might want to go and
get yours.' And he said, 'Mine?' Like he didn't know

what I was talking about. He said, 'I don't got no
money. What're you talking about?' And I said, 'That
money you got hid you come out of jail to get.' And he
said, 'I don't got no money hid. I came out cause I
couldn't stand to stay in' — and laughed like he done,
so I knew he was lying. I said, 'Where's your home at
in Oconee? You from town?' I figured that's where he
hid the money. And he said, 'Oconee? I ain't from
Oconee. I'm from right here.' He was born and raised
in this county. Reason his momma died in Oconee, she
was living with her sister, and they buried her there.
That's when I knew he had it on him, all the money
he stole and buried, it was right there beside me, only
difference was he had it not me, and he was fixing to
leave if he could.

JAMES TERRY CREWS: I didn't know what that
meant, but she said it was stolen already and buried
nine years and besides they're all dead anyway . . .

OLETTA CREWS, *interrupting*: I said I'd tell it.
Each word is heavy with its own weight.

*James Terry Crews does not look at her. He does not
answer.*

OLETTA CREWS, *continuing*: And that's when he
said, 'How about some supper?' And I said, 'You
talking to me?' And he said, 'I was. I ain't now' — and
laughed like it was some kind of joke. He said, 'You
look like you might be hungry. How about you and me
eating something?' And I said, 'I don't cook. I'm
retired.' And he said, 'Retired? What're you retired
from?' And I said, 'The human race.' That took him
back. And he said, 'Lord God. I thought you had to be
dead for that.' And I said, 'Some do. Your momma,
maybe.' And he said, 'Don't talk about my momma.
She's some kind of saint in heaven when you rot in
hell.' And I said, 'I don't believe in saints.' And he said
he didn't care. He knew her I didn't and started doing

these things on his head like he was beating up on himself. Show how he did.

James Terry Crews slaps at his forehead, then at his ears, first with one hand then with the other. It looks like some sort of ritual gesture — a fractured sign of the cross or mea culpa.

OLETTA CREWS: When I saw him do that, I said, 'What you do that for?' And he said it was something he learned in prison. Means you're sorry for what you done. And I said, 'What for?' And he said, 'Whatever. It works for all.'

JAMES TERRY CREWS: I thought he was crazy.

OLETTA CREWS: Me too. I figured he was going to kill us both or else stay here and keep us for ransom.

JAMES TERRY CREWS: What she means is hostages.

OLETTA CREWS: That's right. Stay with us here till he was safe and then kill us as soon as he walked out that door, going to California.

JAMES TERRY CREWS: She wants to die in California.

OLETTA CREWS: That's right. I'm a poor old woman. That's my only hope, to see California and die happy there. That's all I want.

JAMES TERRY CREWS: That's all she wants.

OLETTA CREWS: They got the Pacific Ocean out there. I got a picture in the bathroom from *National Geographic.* You ever see that one on California? That picture I got's the best one in it. I see that picture, I get all smooth inside. The jitters fall off like leaves off a tree. Shows the ocean and the sun going down, smooth and calm as far as the eye can see. Another thing — it don't ever rain. There ain't no rain of terror out there. Nature is mild. They got orange trees, bloom all year, and you want an orange, you pick it yourself.

JAMES TERRY CREWS: They got retirement.

Oletta Crews turns and stares at him. James Terry Crews falls silent.

OLETTA CREWS: What he was saying is they take care of you out there even if you don't got no children.

JAMES TERRY CREWS: I got a daughter.

OLETTA CREWS, *shouting*: There ain't no minimum social security. No matter how much you made, they fix it up so you live like a prince. It ain't like here. They care about you in California. All it takes is getting out there. You got a bus ticket to California, you got a ticket to the Garden of Eden. It's like what they call your Heart's Desire.

JAMES TERRY CREWS: They know all that. Tell them what happened.

OLETTA CREWS: That's what I'm trying to do — *as though blaming him for the interruption.* He was going to California and we stopped him, that's all. *She stops suddenly as though slamming a door:* We already told the police.

JAMES TERRY CREWS: That was yesterday. This is today.

OLETTA CREWS: What do I care? I'm old. *Pauses.* I said, 'Fix your own dinner. I'm too old.'

JAMES TERRY CREWS: I fixed it for him.

OLETTA CREWS: He fixed it.

JAMES TERRY CREWS: I told him I'd fix it. I said, 'I generally fix the meals around here.'

OLETTA CREWS: And he said, 'You know how to cook?' *She turns to her husband*: I'm telling this. He said, 'You know how to cook?' like he was surprised at a man cooking. And I said, 'How you think you ate in prison?' And he said, 'With my hands. Haw, haw.' And I said, 'I thought you might have used a spoon.' That straightened him up. And then I said, 'He learned in the army,' meaning James Terry Crews. He was in the second world war and cooked for generals when he wasn't killing folks.

JAMES TERRY CREWS: I cooked for General Eisenhower. *The memory seems to stir the ashes in James Terry Crews, and he comes back to life.* I cooked steak and eggs for breakfast, and he drank whisky. He didn't touch a drop of coffee. He said, 'I'll have whisky, Cookie. You got some Bourbon?' And I said 'Damn right. I'll make it myself.' I didn't even know what I was talking about. He was the most famous man in the world. This was overseas in France.

OLETTA CREWS: They don't want to hear about that. That's too long ago, and he's dead anyway. They want to hear about Q.B. Farris.

JAMES TERRY CREWS: He's dead.

OLETTA CREWS: He died more recent.

James Terry Crews turns away.

OLETTA CREWS: Now, where was I?

JAMES TERRY CREWS: Cooking dinner.

OLETTA CREWS: You were out cooking dinner —
and I was entertaining him. I asked what he robbed to
get in a work camp for eighteen years. I figured it
must have been a bank. And he said, 'Robbed? Who
told you that?' And I said, 'I don't need nobody to tell
me nothing. I can figure it out by myself.' And he said,
'Then in that case you tell me.' And I said, 'A bank. I
figure you for robbing a bank.' That's when it came to
me. If he robbed a bank, there must have been a lot of
money. Where was the suitcase? I said, 'You got a car?'
And he said, 'Not yet.' And I said, 'How'd you get
here?' And he said, 'Through the woods. I walked.'
Pauses. That's when I knew he had it on him,
thousands of dollars wrapped up in plastic inside his
pocket. And I said, 'You going to California?' And he
said, 'Not if I can stay with you, momma. I love you
too much to go off and leave you.'

JAMES TERRY CREWS: Then we ate dinner, and I
told him about the army. He said it sounded a lot like
prison, and I told him he was wrong about that.
There's a world of difference between them, I said.

OLETTA CREWS: They just talked about this and
that. Most of it him and the other one. I didn't listen. I
was thinking about what comes next. And then I asked
him, 'Are we prisoners?' And he said, 'Not any more
than I am.' And I said, 'What's that supposed to mean?'

JAMES TERRY CREWS: That was what you might
call a threat.

OLETTA CREWS: A threat?

JAMES TERRY CREWS: Meaning we were hostages.

OLETTA CREWS: That's right. We were hostages. It
was a threat.

JAMES TERRY CREWS: Then we finished supper.

OLETTA CREWS: We finished supper, and he said, 'Here, let me help you.' And I said, 'Help what?' And he said, 'Clean up. Don't you clean up the dishes? You let them stay dirty, or you got dogs?' And I said, 'Dogs? What dogs got to do with it?' And he said, A joke. He was joking. He was a jokey fellow, he said. And I said, 'I don't see nothing funny about dogs.' And he said he meant lick the dishes, clean them that way. And I said, 'James Terry does the dishes, and besides that I never had a dog in my life. Dogs unclean. It says in the Bible.' Then I told him they don't have dogs in California. And he said, 'California? You ever been there?' And I said, 'Not yet. I'm fixing to.'

JAMES TERRY CREWS: As soon as she can sell this place. She's been talking about it ever since she retired. Going to California, I told him, that's where she wants to go and die happy.

OLETTA CREWS: And he laughed at that. I said, 'What are you laughing at? That some kind of joke like dogs?' And he said, 'No ma'am. I was thinking about dying happy.' I didn't even look at him. I told my husband, I said, 'You better clean up the dishes before he calls in some dogs to do it.' And he laughed and made like he was going to hug me, but I flung him off, and he said, 'That's why I like you, momma. You're so fast and full of jokes.'

JAMES TERRY CREWS: Then we went and washed the dishes. He called me dad.

OLETTA CREWS: Same way he called me momma. He didn't mean it.

JAMES TERRY CREWS: Tell them about the dictionary.

OLETTA CREWS: I sat right here and tried to read the dictionary. *She reaches under the sofa and pulls out a book, the covers missing, the pages dirty and dog-eared.* This is the dictionary. I was reading it.

JAMES TERRY CREWS: Reads it all day, that and the Bible, when she ain't watching television. That's what she does.

OLETTA CREWS: It's all in there, everything you need to know. One's the head and the other's the heart. I got something to figure out, I read the dictionary till I find what it is.

JAMES TERRY CREWS: The Bible's the heart. She reads it to ease her heart.

OLETTA CREWS: When it gets too full. But I couldn't find it. *She seems eager to talk.* It was there, but I couldn't find it.

JAMES TERRY CREWS: Find what?

OLETTA CREWS: What comes next. And then it came to me. I was in the bathroom, and I heard them washing the dishes and talking, and I was looking out at the ocean, that picture I told you about of the water. That's when it came to me.

JAMES TERRY CREWS: That's when she decided.

OLETTA CREWS: I didn't decide. Something told me.

JAMES TERRY CREWS: Something told her.

OLETTA CREWS: Like a voice in California. I got up and flushed the toilet and went back and sat down and turned it over in my mind.

Oletta Crews holds up her hand.

OLETTA CREWS: Listen to me. This is the main part. I knew what he was fixing to do, and he knew I knew. I heard that where God led me this far on TV, and now he was telling me what to do next.

JAMES TERRY CREWS: God. The voice she heard, it was God.

OLETTA CREWS: They know that. Who else got a voice? Of course it was God, speaks in your heart just like he led me on TV to know who it was came to the door in the rain of terror. And he opened it — *indicating her husband* — and I looked out and knew who it was like in a mirror, he looked so familiar.

JAMES TERRY CREWS, *prompting*: You were afraid.

OLETTA CREWS: Yes.

JAMES TERRY CREWS: You killed him because you were afraid.

OLETTA CREWS: Yes. *And then:* I didn't kill him.

JAMES TERRY CREWS: I killed him.

OLETTA CREWS, *shouting*: Don't listen to him. Listen to me. He don't know nothing.

JAMES TERRY CREWS, *explaining to the audience*: I don't know nothing.

OLETTA CREWS: He just did it. I heard the voice.

JAMES TERRY CREWS, *explaining*: She heard the voice. I'm the one murdered him.

OLETTA CREWS, *shouting*: It wasn't a murder. The police said that. They say, 'You shoot whoever you want to, Lady, breaks in your house and keeps you hostage.'

JAMES TERRY CREWS: Damn right, wouldn't you? *Explaining*: She was afraid he might kill her.

OLETTA CREWS: Yes, and I was afraid he might kill him too — *indicating her husband*. I need him to help me. Besides, I heard the voice. It spoke in my heart. *And then she stops as though reflecting*. You can't serve two masters. That's what it said. "No man can serve two masters: for either he will hate the one, and love the other; or else he will hold to the one and despise the other." I thought how to do it.

JAMES TERRY CREWS: How to kill him.

OLETTA CREWS: I thought of ways how to do it. Like roach tablets, putting them in his grits at breakfast, and then I thought, What if they don't work? What if they just work on roaches? Then I thought of rat poison. But what if it tastes funny? Draino. That's too strong. Lysol and Clorox. He might have to drink a gallon. Poison is out.

JAMES TERRY CREWS: I told her about the nail.

OLETTA CREWS: That was later, when he went to bed.

JAMES TERRY CREWS, *begins*: In the ear . . .

OLETTA CREWS, *shouting*: It was all over by then. I already figured it out. He said, 'What about a nail?' And I said 'A nail?' And he said, 'I read about it in the paper.'

JAMES TERRY CREWS: No, I didn't. It was in the *Police Gazette*, in the Charlotte, North Carolina, bus station. I was waiting, and I went to the newsstand

and picked up the magazines like you do, looking for pictures . . .

OLETTA CREWS: They got pictures of half-naked women where they been raped in the *Police Gazette.* That's what he was looking at.

JAMES TERRY CREWS: No, I wasn't. I was just looking, waiting for time to pass till I got my bus, and I picked up the *Police Gazette*, and the first thing I turn to, that was it. Nail Murder. All about how this farmer in Kansas and this girl friend he got killed her husband by driving a thirty penny nail in his ear. *James Terry Crews glances about.* They killed him by driving a nail in his ear — *leaning forward.* You know why they did that?

OLETTA CREWS, *breaking in, shouting*: So it wouldn't be a wound. They know that. That nail went in, and they wiped up the blood and burned the rag and called the doctor and said, 'He rose up in the bed and shouted and fell over dead.' And the doctor didn't even look in the ear. Said, 'Must have been a heart attack.' And they almost got away with it except for the farmer. He went crazy and confessed it all. Otherwise they'd have joined the farms, his and the one she got from the murder, and made a million dollars by now selling it off for shopping centers.

JAMES TERRY CREWS: You ever hear anything like that? That's what you call a perfect crime, except he went crazy.

OLETTA CREWS: That's where he went wrong. That's why it ain't perfect. So I told him the nail was out. *Intimately to the audience*: I even thought of cutting his throat. Waiting till he was asleep and then creep in the light at the end of the hall shining in so we could see the vein in his neck beating and then pull the razor across it. But what if the gristle was too hard to cut through? I ain't that strong, and I knew he couldn't do it — *indicating her husband*. He can talk about nails all he wants to, but he couldn't even hold it still. He's too soft. He might look at him and feel sorry for him. I couldn't chance it. I didn't want Duke getting up, throat flapping open from ear to ear where I cut at it and him not dead. Ain't no telling what he might do, bleeding like that, bubbling and shouting. He'd kill me for sure. That's when I knew James Terry would have to shoot him.

JAMES TERRY CREWS: I had to. You heard her.

OLETTA CREWS, *shouting*: Hold on. Don't rush ahead. They ain't finished the dishes yet. I got out of the bathroom and they came in and sat down, and James Terry said, 'Duke's been telling me about all the good times they had in the work camp. He liked it there.' And I said, 'If he liked it so much, why didn't he stay? Why come around here bothering us?' And then he says, 'What's on TV? And I said, 'Nothing.' And he says, 'They got Monday Night Football?' And I said, 'I don't watch it. I don't know the rules.' And he said, 'What about you, old dad?' — meaning my husband, James Terry Crews.

JAMES TERRY CREWS: I said I don't watch it either. It's too rough.

OLETTA CREWS: That's right. I told him, 'That game's all right for the work camp,' I said. 'Rough men done worse than that to each other every day of their lives, but it ain't all right for women and children. It's too rough. Besides which,' I told him, 'it ain't Monday night.' And he said, 'Not Monday?' And I said, 'That's right. Yesterday was Monday. This is Tuesday.' And he laughed at that and said, 'Lord God,' and grinned like he just ate something he shouldn't.

JAMES TERRY CREWS: He had this kind of shit-eating grin.

OLETTA CREWS: It was attractive. I don't mean that. He said, 'I can keep up with it in the work camp. It's when I get out. That's when I lose track.' And I said, 'How many times you get out?' And he said every chance he got. That and Monday Night Football's his only pleasure, he said, that and beating up on folks to get in the work camp in the first place. 'And grinning,' I said. 'You left out grinning.' And he laughed and said, 'That's right, momma. That's the only pleasure I got, that and being here with you. What about going to bed?' And I thought this is when the raping commences. And I said, 'Not me. I don't go to bed and get raped.' And you know what he did? *Pauses.* He laughed. *Indignantly:* He fell on the floor like he couldn't stand up and kicked his feet in the air, pretending. Looked like the devil come up through the floor from hell. And he said, 'Momma, you ever think you gonna get raped, you know what I'd do?' But I didn't answer. I was too ashamed, and he laughed and said, 'I'd stay up instead. I'd stay up all night before I'd go to bed and get raped.' And so on like that. But I didn't look at him. I heard him scrabbling around down there at my feet, but I didn't dare cast my eyes on him to see what nasty things he was doing.

JAMES TERRY CREWS: He was getting up.

OLETTA CREWS: I didn't want to see what it was for fear it might be something I didn't want to. That's how he was. He didn't care. Then I felt him lean over me grinning and mocking, and say what he meant was for me to go to one bed and him to another and sleep this time, if that was all right with me. And that's when I knew there wasn't no way. Even if I could have saved him before, I knew I couldn't after that. *Pauses.* I was a prisoner in my own house.

JAMES TERRY CREWS, *intimately to the audience:*

He trusted us. He said, 'I sleep light, but I trust you anyway, old dad. I know you don't want me to go back to the work camp for nine more years. And he said to Mrs. Crews, 'Wake me for breakfast you hear me, momma? Don't let me oversleep my welcome. I'm just going to rest a minute. Then I'm going to have to leave you, much as you hate to see me go.'

OLETTA CREWS, *shouting*: And I thought then, to California. He's going to California without me and leave me alone and take all the money. And that's when I told James Terry to kill him. I said, 'Go get your gun.'

JAMES TERRY CREWS: I got this single barrel shotgun. First gun I ever owned.

OLETTA CREWS: They don't want to hear that.

JAMES TERRY CREWS: Let me talk. This is interesting. I got that gun in Fayetteville when I was a boy. Walked in and slapped down seven dollars and said, 'I'll take that Stevens single barrel,' and Mr. Robert said, 'This squirrel gun?' And I said, 'Squirrel gun? I could bring you down with it if I had some buckshot.' That's the way I was then. I didn't take no smart talk from nobody. And he said, 'What you fixing to shoot with it if you don't shoot me?' And I said, 'I don't know' — like I was still thinking about it. I said, 'I ain't made up my mind yet.' And then I said, 'Give me some buckshot.' That straightened him up. Buckshot'll blow a hole in a man big as a melon. He looked at me, and he wasn't smiling. I was a man when I was fourteen, when I first went to work for the sawmill. I worked there till I hurt myself and moved to Atlanta and got married and went to painting. But I kept that gun. I had others, but it was my favorite. It reminded me . . .

OLETTA CREWS, *shouting*: That's beside the point.

The point is I could say, Go in there and do it, and James Terry would go in there and I'd feel it shake when he shot at him once — twice — three times maybe, in the head and in the back, wherever it hits him. But what then? He'd be laying in my bed, and he'd bleed on it and ruin the mattress.

JAMES TERRY CREWS: Not to mention the shot. She didn't even think about that. Blood ain't nothing. Blood washes off. But buckshot — buckshot'll blow a hole in a man big as a melon through him and the mattress both. Might even blow a hole in the floor. *His face lights up.* I ever tell you about the time we were moving, and there was a copperhead in the house, and I had the gun, but the shells were packed up somewhere in boxes?

OLETTA CREWS: Don't be an idiot.

JAMES TERRY CREWS: I shot a hole in the floor — *hurrying to the end.* I found the shells and shot the floor clean out. Snake with it. *He looks at his wife. Stubbornly:* Ever see buckshot hit a melon?

OLETTA CREWS: Hush up. You're talking too much.

JAMES TERRY CREWS, *turning to face the audience:* It explodes. You can't even find the pieces. It just lifts and disappears. Same way with heads.

OLETTA CREWS: I knew I'd smell it. Whenever I put my face to it, I knew I'd smell it in my sleep no matter how good I washed it. The police would come and take off the body, but they'd leave all the blood in the mattress and on the sheets and on the rugs across the floor where it runs out when they carry him off, and I'd have to clean it up. He can't clean — *indicating her husband.* All he can do is paint.

JAMES TERRY CREWS, *joyously*: I say paint it. If it's dirty enough to wash it, it's dirty enough to paint it, I say.

OLETTA CREWS: Only trouble is you can't paint sheets and mattresses where all the blood ran out. *To audience*: If it wasn't drinking it was talking. All his life. He'd get to painting a house and talk himself right off the job. Couldn't even climb the ladder or mix the paint, he talked so much. Folks don't like that. They run him off, and it wasn't even drinking sometimes. It's what he calls high spirits.

James Terry Crews looks at her balefully, with sore eyes.

JAMES TERRY CREWS: High spirits.

OLETTA CREWS: Besides which I thought of something else. What about Q.B. Farris? Where was his gun? And what about the money? What if he had it in his pocket, and James Terry shot it all full of holes? Would they still take it? What do they do with money like that?

JAMES TERRY CREWS: They don't do nothing cause it blows away just like a melon. If he had that money in his pocket, you couldn't even find the pieces.

OLETTA CREWS: That's what I thought. Besides, he can't see in the daytime let alone in the dark, at night. He might point it at Duke's head and hit the wrong place and just wound him and he come crawling out at me.

JAMES TERRY CREWS: That's why I picked up the other two loads — in case I missed. I ain't never shot a man before.

OLETTA CREWS: He said he might miss the first,

but not the second. But I told him 'No. It's too dangerous. There's some other way.' And he said, 'I can't think of it.' And I said, 'I know. I wasn't expecting you to. Give me a minute.' *Pauses.* 'Even though I walk through the valley of the shadow of death, I fear no evil, for thou art with me.' And then it said, 'It ain't your death. That's why it's a shadow. If it was yours it'd be real. But killing him's only a shadow.' And as soon as I heard that, I knew who it was, and all my fear fell off like sweat, and I dried up, it's like I was reborn. I knew what was promised. And I said to James Terry, 'Let it go. Don't shoot him now. Wait till later.' And he said, 'When?' And I said, 'Later, when he's fixing to kill us.'

JAMES TERRY CREWS, *nervously*: And I said, 'What if it's too late. What if he beats me to it?' And she said, 'Then you don't have to worry. You'll be already dead by then.' That don't make no sense to me.

OLETTA CREWS: And I said, 'It won't come to that. Just get it loaded. I'll give you a sign — like this.' *She winks her eye and waves her hand.*

JAMES TERRY CREWS: And I said, 'What if I'm tying my shoe and don't see you do it? What if I get up and go to the bathroom?'

OLETTA CREWS, *ignoring him:* We heard him rattling around in there, and I said, 'Get ready. He's fixing to kill us.' And James Terry said, 'What do I do?' And I said, 'Sit here.' *She pats the cushion beside her.* 'And hide the gun under the sofa where you can get at it.'

JAMES TERRY CREWS: And I said, 'That's too slow. He'll shoot us both before I get to it.' And she said, 'That's all right. In that case you don't got nothing to worry about.'

OLETTA CREWS, *shouting*: All my fear dried up like sweat.

JAMES TERRY CREWS: And I cocked it and put it under the sofa. There ain't no safety on a single barrel Stevens . . .

OLETTA CREWS: They don't want to hear about that. We were sitting here on the sofa waiting.

JAMES TERRY CREWS: Not me. I was thinking about what if he kills me. That worried me.

OLETTA CREWS: And always will. That's what's wrong with you. *Long pause.* We heard him stirring and singing, and then he came in tucking James Terry's shirt in his pants where he hid the gun and stopped and fell back all of a sudden like he was surprised, and said, 'I didn't see you sitting there. You almost scared me to death' — grinning and laughing to show he was lying. He tried to hug me, but I pushed him off. And then he said, 'I got to go, much as I hate to leave you, momma.'

JAMES TERRY CREWS: And I said, 'Why don't you stay then? What's your hurry?' I didn't mind him so much. He wasn't so bad, except he might kill us. He had a good heart. Then I saw her look at me, and I felt my bowels tighten up. They were feeling loose . . .

OLETTA CREWS, *ignoring him*: And then Duke said, 'I'd sure like to stay, old dad. It feels just like home.' And I said, 'Home? It ain't your home. I don't want children. I never had them.' And he laughed at that and said, 'I know. I'd have guessed that from how you kept your figure even if you hadn't told me about it. You sure look good for a woman your age' — laughing and grinning so I didn't know if he meant it or not. And I tried to hit him. I said, 'Go on. Don't talk like that. My husband's sitting right here beside me.'

JAMES TERRY CREWS: And I said, 'Don't mind me. I think she's pretty good looking myself.'

OLETTA CREWS: And then he said, 'They'll be along soon looking for me. Don't tell them I been here.' I don't want to go back to the work camp. I'd rather be dead than go back there the rest of my life. How would you like it?' And I said, 'I wouldn't. But I wouldn't deserve to.' That straightened him up. And he said, 'Well, I gotta go. Much obliged for the company. It ain't often I get to have such high times.'

JAMES TERRY CREWS: And I said, 'Me neither. I enjoyed it.' I said, 'Come back. You ever get where they ain't looking for you, come back. You know where it's at. Come and stay. We'd like to have you. You're good company.'

OLETTA CREWS: I didn't say nothing. And he said, 'How about you? You want me to come back too, momma?' And I said, 'I won't be here. I'm fixing to go to California.' Then his face fell, and he looked old. He said, 'I sure do wish you luck,' — reaching over to shake James Terry by the hand. And he said to me, 'I know how you feel wanting to go someplace like California.'

JAMES TERRY CREWS: Then he slapped me on the shoulder and hugged me and said, 'I might buy this mobile home myself.'

OLETTA CREWS: That's how I knew he had the money. He wasn't lying.

JAMES TERRY CREWS: He'd a done it if he had the time.

OLETTA CREWS: And the money. That's when I told him I might see him there. And he said, 'Where?' And I said, 'California.' And he grinned and said, 'You might do it.' Then he looked at me. He looked me right in the eye and said, 'I'll see you in California, momma.' And I knew then I was right. He's fixing to walk out that door and shut it behind him and then creep back when we're sitting here on the sofa thinking he's gone now, the danger is over, our lives in our own hands again, praising God and weeping for joy we ain't dead, he didn't kill us after all, when all of a sudden the door flings open, and there he is standing there grinning and laughing like a devil from hell cause it's a joke, don't you see, pretending to leave and then coming back and shooting us both right on the sofa side by side, one after the other — Bang, bang, bang — till it wasn't even a sofa no more, just a hole in the floor and us in it, bits and pieces mixed with the stuffing.

JAMES TERRY CREWS, *correcting her*: That's a shotgun. You're talking about a twelve gauge shotgun.

OLETTA CREWS: That was his plan. I saw it as clear as I'm seeing you, and I knew I was right. That's just like him, I thought to myself — kill us like we were some kind of joke. You ain't got no will if you're a hostage. You have to sit there and wait.

JAMES TERRY CREWS: Unless you kill him first. That's right, ain't it Letta?

OLETTA CREWS: It's like you can't move. You ain't got no will of your own.

JAMES TERRY CREWS: That's what I mean. That's why I killed him. No matter how good a heart he had, he was conceited.

OLETTA CREWS: And I said, 'Ain't you scared?' And he said, 'What for?' I didn't know if he was joking or not. I said, 'There's a posse of police out there waiting.' And he said, 'What for?' like he didn't know

what I was talking about and went to the door and
stuck his head out like he was trying to see who was
out there. And I said, 'Cause you don't care. You joke
too much. You ain't serious.'

JAMES TERRY CREWS, *agreeing*: He was
conceited. I could see that.

OLETTA CREWS: I made the sign. And James
Terry reached under and got the shotgun, and Duke
turned around and looked at James Terry, and James
Terry looked at Duke, and then his head lifted off. If it
weren't for the roaring in my ears and the light and
the smoke and the shaking on the sofa beside me
where James Terry shot it off, I'd have thought it
busted or something, like a balloon. One minute it was
Duke Farris, the next minute it was gone, like it went
out the door. *Pauses.* It was still raining, and I thought
to myself, it ain't there. It ain't out there. You can look
all you want to, but there ain't even bits and pieces. It
lifted clean off. That head exploded. *She pauses.* I was
glad the door was open. That way it went right out. It
didn't blow a hole in the wall, and there wasn't
nothing left to clean up. I said, 'Help me up.' And he
didn't move, I got up and went over there, and you
know what he had in his pockets? A ring snap off an
aluminum can. He didn't even have a wallet. If he was
hit by a car on the highway and killed on the spot, you
wouldn't have even known who it was. I searched
everywhere, and I told my husband, I said, 'James
Terry, I can't find the money.' I couldn't believe it.
And he said, 'What money?' And I said, 'That money
he was going to California with. The money he hid and
came out to dig up.' And James Terry said, 'Where is
it?' I said, 'I don't know. You shot him too soon.'

JAMES TERRY CREWS: He didn't even have a gun.

OLETTA CREWS: He didn't have nothing except a
ring snap off an aluminum can. But how was I to

know that? The police said, 'Don't worry. You shot him on your own property.' And I said, 'My own property? I shot him in my own house. How was I to know?' And they said, 'No way. He might have had a gun to kill you.'

JAMES TERRY CREWS: That's probably even my ring snap off an aluminum can. He was wearing my pants. There wasn't nothing in his at all.

OLETTA CREWS: Police said it was self-defense. Said, 'You killed him to save yourself. That's only natural.'

JAMES TERRY CREWS: Ain't a jury in the land convict you of that.

OLETTA CREWS: I couldn't move it. I sat down on the floor beside the body and tried to push it out with my feet. I wanted to close the door. It was still raining. I said to James Terry, 'I can't move it by myself. Get up and help.' And he got up. Then I saw him lift an arm and start to drag him out. A leg slid by me and then a foot, and then I was free. *Pauses.* The door was open, and I looked out and saw the rain. The floodlight was still on. It went out in the yard like a room and lit up the rain. I could see it coming down like knives. It was all silver, and in the tree, it was all silver like ice — like the whole world turned to ice. And James Terry started to come in, and I said, 'Get the light.' And he got the light, and it was dark. It was dark out there as far as the eye could see, and I could still hear it raining. It was like it was moving, like a great wind lifting and heaving. And I said to James Terry, 'Close the door. Close the door on it.' And he closed the door.

JAMES TERRY CREWS: He wasn't so bad. I don't care what they say he did, he had a good heart. Lots of folks rob banks got better hearts than the people that own them. He was what you might call a godsend.

OLETTA CREWS, *savagely*: We were hostages. He took our will.

JAMES TERRY CREWS: I mean before that.

OLETTA CREWS: There wasn't no before that.

JAMES TERRY CREWS: I mean when we were doing the dishes. I thought to myself, I wouldn't be here laughing and talking and cutting the fool if he wasn't here. I'm grateful to him.

OLETTA CREWS: Listen to me. I know about godsend. As soon as I heard that knock on the door, I felt it knocking in my heart, I said to myself, it's God knocking at the door of my heart, asking me to open up and let him come in and change me. Change my whole life. There's a better place than this, and I thought I was going. But I know better now even if he don't - *indicating James Terry Crews. She turns to the audience and changes her voice, increasing its intensity. It is as though someone else is speaking inside her*: "For even Satan disguises himself as an angel of light. His end shall be according to his deeds." And his shows that when James Terry shot him and there wasn't no money.

JAMES TERRY CREWS: And no gun.

OLETTA CREWS: And nothing to show, except mockery. All my hopes mocked and bleeding half in and half out the door where I couldn't even shut it myself, and he dragged it out where it'd been killed. I felt like something inside me was dead.

JAMES TERRY CREWS: Me too. I felt like something was dead inside me too. I didn't know what it was.

OLETTA CREWS: I did. I sat on the floor where I'd

been looking for money, and I thought to myself, 'You can't serve two masters.' Satan appeared as an angel of light and killed all my hopes, took my will and killed all my hopes, but I'm still alive. *Pauses.* I ain't dead, and I ain't changed. I'm just like I was.

Darkness. The sound of rain. Distant music.

An Errand of Mercy

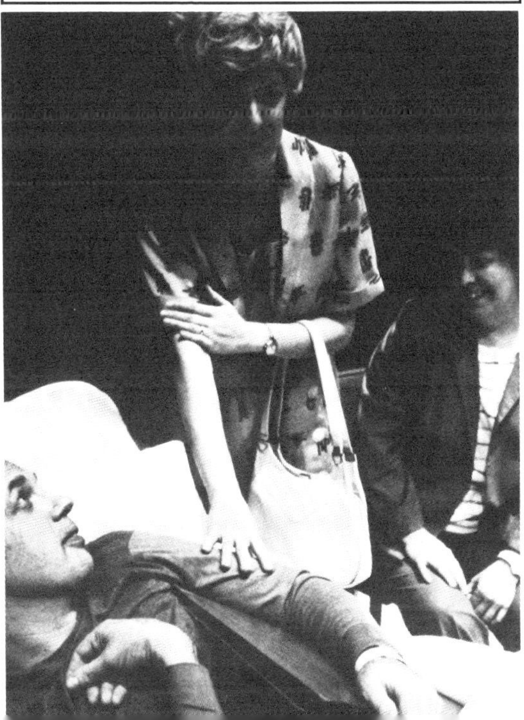

CAST OF CHARACTERS

ORA BELLE IVEY, a retired schoolteacher
RUBY UPCHURCH, a widow
RAY BURGESS, a nursing home resident

The sound of music as though at a distance. At first it is barely perceptible, then gradually grows louder and louder until it is present, immediate.

The stage is in darkness except for the obscure blue light of a television set. In the light one sees a vast, empty chamber, the only feature being a hospital bed and in it a figure who seems no larger than a child or small ape dressed in a hospital gown and ski cap. The figure stares straight ahead and rolls rhythmically from hip to hip. The only other thing in the room is a metal chair that serves as a table — things piled on the seat, a blue towel thrown on top. The light centers only on the bed. The rest of the room seems to extend indefinitely into the shadows. The impression is that of immense sparsity and emptiness, not threatening, but featureless — a sense of sameness, boredom: one of the more subtle forms of despair.

The music fades and we hear two voices speaking as though from outside the room.

As the play begins and the two women enter the room, it is immediately clear that one of them defers to the other. She is more tentative by nature, younger (but not by much), slimmer, wearing clothes that seem curiously dated, as though they might have been worn for years, but only on special occasions. She seems eager to make a good impression but uncertain of how to go about it. She has no public manner, giving the impression of having led a rich emotional life within a small circle of family and friends. To everyone else she was hidden, unknown, never at ease, never fully herself. Now, after thirty or forty years of relative isolation, she is like a woman returning to work after raising a family. She is not only inexperienced, she is trusting and childlike. The only difference between her and a child is that she knows what she is.

If the younger woman knows herself too well, the other one knows nothing about herself at all. She is neatly dressed in country clothes, with stout shoes like a man's, hair cropped short, ruddy complexion. She looks like an androgynous farmer. Her voice is loud with assurance, and as she speaks, she tends to shout, not because she is hard of hearing, but because she is certain of her own rectitude and the justness of her opinions. She carries herself like one of the elect already given a white suffrage. Compared with her the other woman is like one of the poor souls in purgatory, suffering for all the venial sins of her life. She is infinitely well meaning and willing to do good if she only knew what it was. The other one knows. She was born knowing.

A sudden burst of light. The two women appear inside it, as though they had just materialized. Then darkness again. They have entered the room.

ORA BELLE IVEY: There he is, but you can't hardly make him out, it's so dark in here. Turn on the light. No wonder he had a stroke and turned into a vegetable.

RUBY UPCHURCH: You mean he's like a vegetable? Ain't that awful?

ORA BELLE IVEY: It's awful all right. But not as bad as it might have been. There's always something worse off than you are. Thank God for that.

RUBY UPCHURCH: What's worse than vegetables?

ORA BELLE IVEY: There's always something. You can be sure of that. Now turn on the light.

Ruby Upchurch finds the light switch behind her.

ORA BELLE IVEY: That's better. And turn off that TV. He don't need it now he got us.

RUBY UPCHURCH: There he is.

The figure in the bed stares straight ahead and continues to roll from hip to hip.
Ruby Upchurch moves toward the TV and turns it off.

ORA BELLE IVEY: What's it say his name is?

RUBY UPCHURCH: What?

ORA BELLE IVEY: That bracelet he got on his wrist so they know who he is if he dies. What's it say?

RUBY UPCHURCH: I don't know.

ORA BELLE IVEY: Go see.

RUBY UPCHURCH: Not me. I couldn't do it.

Ora Belle Ivey walks toward the bed and lifts the wrist. Ray Burgess, *she reads, letting the arm fall from her hand. It hits the edge of the mattress and bounces.*

ORA BELLE IVEY, *shouting as into a deep well:*
Ray Burgess.

RUBY UPCHURCH: You reckon he hears us?

ORA BELLE IVEY: We don't know. That's the

trouble. How're you going to do an errand of mercy if the one you're doing it to don't know you're doing it? How you going to cheer him up that way? He can't talk. We know that for a fact . . . .

RUBY UPCHURCH: That don't mean he can't hear.

Ray Burgess stops rolling back and forth. Only his eyes continue the motion, shifting from one of the women toward the other.

RUBY UPCHURCH: Look it there. He got his eyes open. Look at him looking.

ORA BELLE IVEY: That's awful ain't it, the way he's looking? Looks like some kind of wild animal. You see that?

RUBY UPCHURCH: I saw it as soon as we came in when it was still dark. One time John and I went to the zoo . . . .

ORA BELLE IVEY: Let the dead bury the dead. You got problems enough right here. We know he can't talk . . .

RUBY UPCHURCH, *interrupting*: But he can see.

ORA BELLE IVEY: That don't mean he can hear. The question is does he know what we're saying. *She turns to Ray Burgess*: Your name is Ray Burgess. *She shouts louder than usual, the way some people try to converse with the deaf or with foreigners.* R—A—Y B—U—R—G—E—S—S — *enunciating every syllable as distinctly as possible. Ray Burgess does not respond.*

ORA BELLE IVEY: He don't look so old does he?

RUBY UPCHURCH: Don't talk about him to his face till you're sure he can't hear us. You might say something you wished you hadn't.

ORA BELLE IVEY: There ain't nothing wrong with not looking old. *Turning to Ray Burgess*: Ray Burgess, I'm Miss Ora Belle Ivey, and this beside me is Mrs. Ruby Upchurch, widow of Mr. John Upchurch, lately deceased. We're here on an errand of mercy on behalf of the Fightingtown Baptist Association to cheer you up and let you know there's something out there beside the nurses' station. We're here to fellowship you and help you forget them that cared so little about you they put you in here to die by yourself. *She pauses to let the significance of what she said sink in.*

RUBY UPCHURCH, *shouting*: Watch out, Ora Belle, he got something under the cover. He's pulling it out.

ORA BELLE IVEY: It's some kind of board with writing on it. An alphabet from A to Z and numbers. It got numbers at the bottom.

RUBY UPCHURCH: A ouija board. He got a ouija board in his bed.

ORA BELLE IVEY: What's that supposed to mean?

RUBY UPCHURCH: We had one when the children were little. You talk on it to the other side.

ORA BELLE IVEY: The other side of what?

RUBY UPCHURCH: The other side of life. You talk to the dead.

ORA BELLE IVEY: The dead?

RUBY UPCHURCH: You ask them questions, spell out what you want to know, and somebody comes, one of the dead, sometimes a loved one. *Her voice sounds distant.* Sometimes the one you loved the most, if they've gone before and they want to reach out and touch you again, you can talk to them. Sometimes they say it's an Indian. The directions say it could be an Indian or a Chinese. They might be dead a thousand years — Romans, Egyptians, one of them.

ORA BELLE IVEY: What about the apostles of Christ?

RUBY UPCHURCH: The directions didn't say nothing about them.

ORA BELLE IVEY: They're dead ain't they? If it calls up the dead, they qualify, don't they? But it didn't say nothing about them. And I'll tell you why. The dead don't talk. Saul drove forth the witches from the land of Canaan, and Jesus himself cast out devils.

RUBY UPCHURCH: And he rose up Lazarus from the dead. *It is as though she is speaking of something else*: He was dead in the tomb I don't know how long, and Jesus came in his infinite mercy and gave him back his life again, and he got up and walked out of that place of death into the light, and he saw his wife, and she knew that he was living again, that God in his infinite mercy gave him back to her.

ORA BELLE IVEY: That's different. That's something entirely different. We ain't talking about miracles. We're talking about something you hide in the bed and slip up under the covers.

RUBY UPCHURCH: It's just a game. *She sounds embarrassed.* The children got it one Christmas. They used to talk to little children.

ORA BELLE IVEY: You mean dead children.

RUBY UPCHURCH: Well, yes. But it was more like talking on the telephone. And the funny thing was —

suddenly brightening — the children they talked to couldn't spell.

ORA BELLE IVEY: Most of them can't. That's been my experience. *And then she cries,* Watch out, *and moves as quickly as she can away from Ray Burgess toward the foot of the bed.* Look it there. He's doing it.

Ray Burgess is holding the board with one hand. The other hand he uses as a pointer, his index finger thin as a chicken's toe indicating letter after letter but not in order as they are written. It is more at random, first this one and now that.

ORA BELLE IVEY: Look at him. Ain't that awful? You reckon he knows what he's doing? *She watches as Ray Burgess' hand moves in patterns.* Is that how you do?

RUBY UPCHURCH: No. That's what's so funny. It takes two. You work it together, and it flows between you.

ORA BELLE IVEY: What flows between you?

RUBY UPCHURCH: The current that calls up the dead. *Laughing suddenly:* What's happening here?

ORA BELLE IVEY: He's calling you forth. That's what's happening. He knows I won't go. My feet are too guarded with angels from all the errands of mercy I been on. He knows he can't tempt me. But you ain't been tested. Besides which you had one of them before, and he knows it. The devil remembers. You called up dead children at Christmas. Look it there. *She touches Ruby Upchurch on the arm as though to restrain her.* Don't go. Stand here with me and harden your heart. Resist him like I do.

Ora Belle Ivey glares at Ray Burgess, and he looks

*back at her. All the while his hands describe motions
of their own against the board. It is as though his eyes
and hands are separate.*

RUBY UPCHURCH: Wait a minute. Look. *Ray
Burgess turns toward her.* Yes, yes. What is it? He's
telling us something.

ORA BELLE IVEY: Who is? That's the problem.
Who's he got on the other side?

RUBY UPCHURCH: What other side?

ORA BELLE IVEY: *The* other side. You said it, not
me. Who's he got there behind that board working it
with him we can't see?

RUBY UPCHURCH: A LUBUM, A LUBUM, A
LUBUM. *Then suddenly*: He's spelling something.
Can't you see that?

ORA BELLE IVEY: Of course I can. I see it all, and I
tell you what. He ain't spelling nothing. *She pauses,
suddenly awestruck*: Unless it ain't him. Unless it's
something else doing the spelling.

RUBY UPCHURCH: A LBUM, A LBUM, A LBUM.
See there. Watch his hand.

ORA BELLE IVEY: I been seeing that. That don't
mean nothing. *She pauses as though slowly filling with
light.* Unless he's speaking in some foreign tongue. It
ain't hello. I'll tell you that. It's something nasty. *She
pauses, brain churning.* It may not even be English.
Ever think that? It may not be nothing in no tongue
known to man. Look now. He's pointing. Oh God, he's
pointing.

*Ray Burgess has dropped his board on his lap and is
pointing toward a chair in a corner, aluminum frame*

and vinyl pad, serving as a table, piled high with a number of things, the most distinct being a blue towel lying on top.

ORA BELLE IVEY: He wants you to sit down. That's what it means, that thing he was saying. Must mean that chair in some foreign tongue.

RUBY UPCHURCH: No. Look there. He's spelling something. T—O. TO something and then the rest.

ORA BELLE IVEY: What's the rest?

RUBY UPCHURCH: W. See there E—L. WEL. TO WEL, it said, TO WEL. What does it mean? *And then she knows.* TOWEL, *she shouts, laughing.* TOWEL. He's saying, TOWEL.

ORA BELLE IVEY: I know that. But what's it mean? What we need is a translator.

RUBY UPCHURCH: It's English. He's saying, Towel, *and she rushes to the chair and lifts the blue towel.* You mean this? *she asks Ray Burgess.*

Ray Burgess nods and rolls about in bed.

ORA BELLE IVEY: Look at him — *seeing Ray Burgess's rhythmical movements.* Look at him. That's disgusting. That's disgusting ain't it, going from side to side like that? Ain't no telling what he's doing.

Ruby Upchurch does not hear. She is caught up in the same excitement as Ray Burgess. Towel, she cries, waving the towel. And then she cries, Album. That's what he meant. Under the towel here's the album. She picks up a book with PHOTOGRAPHS written across the front. It's a photograph album. That's what he meant. It's like writing. He writes out what he wants to say.

Ray Burgess's hand flickers across the board as she speaks, moving back and forth to the corner of the board where the word YES is written.

RUBY UPCHURCH: See there. He's saying, YES. Don't you see that?

ORA BELLE IVEY: Unless it's just twitching. *And then she stops, watching Ruby Upchurch and Ray Burgess.*

RUBY UPCHURCH, *to Ray Burgess*: Do you want the album?

Ray Burgess' hand gestures YES and he nods his head in affirmation. Ruby Upchurch picks up the photograph album and puts the blue towel down in its place. Then she carries the album to Ray Burgess, who opens it in his lap and gestures toward her. LOOK, his hand says moving across the board.

RUBY UPCHURCH, *interrupting*: He says LOOK. He wants us to look.

ORA BELLE IVEY: Do what?

Her mind has been far away watching the simple, familiar gestures of Ruby Upchurch — picking the book up, putting down the towel, carrying the book to Ray Burgess. They move easily together.

ORA BELLE IVEY, *half to herself*: You look like you think you're married or something the way you do that. Makes me feel bad just being here — nasty or something.

RUBY UPCHURCH, *including her*: Come look. He wants us to see his picture album. Come stand here beside us.

Ora Belle Ivey goes forth.

RUBY UPCHURCH: You can't see from there. Come in closer. There. That's better. *Turning to Ray Burgess*: We're ready. What you got there? *She has the gift of intimacy.*

Ray Burgess opens the cover of the book.

ORA BELLE IVEY: It's a cat. I knew it. Look there. He got a picture of a cat. A whole page of them. O God, it got blue eyes, just like a baby.

Ray Burgess' hand flies over the board: SIAMESE.

RUBY UPCHURCH, *interpreting*: Siamese. He says it's Siamese.

ORA BELLE IVEY: Blue eyes on a cat's unnatural. That shows where it comes from.

RAY BURGESS, *describing a word*: NEWARK.

RUBY UPCHURCH: NEWARK.

ORA BELLE IVEY: New what?

RAY BURGESS: NJ.

RUBY UPCHURCH, *reading aloud*: N—J. *Then her face lights up*: New Jersey. Newark, New Jersey. That's where you got the cat. Is that right?

RAY BURGESS: YES, YES — *hand moving back and forth to the corner of the board.*

ORA BELLE IVEY: That's what he says. There ain't but one place blue-eyed cats come from, and it ain't Newark, New Jersey. God never made a blue-eyed animal. That means that cat came from a human.

RUBY UPCHURCH: What do you mean?

ORA BELLE IVEY: They mate with them — men, devils. I don't know which. Cats and people — all mixed together.

RAY BURGESS: NO, NO — *hand moving back and forth, until Ruby Upchurch stills it with hers.*

RUBY UPCHURCH: What's your cat's name? It sure is pretty.

RAY BURGESS: OPAL.

RUBY UPCHURCH: Its name is Opal.

ORA BELLE IVEY, *suspiciously*: That's some kind of car, ain't it?

RAY BURGESS: JEWEL.

RUBY UPCHURCH: He says it means jewel.

RAY BURGESS: FIRE.

RUBY UPCHURCH, *translating*: FIRE. He says it got fire in it. He says his cat is full of fire. That's why you called her Opal, ain't it, because of that fire?

RAY BURGESS: YES, YES.

ORA BELLE IVEY, *suspiciously*: It all goes together.

RUBY UPCHURCH: Look it there, *pointing to the album.* Look at that cat. See how she's laying there in that chair? Look at her feet.

ORA BELLE IVEY: That's disgusting. You or me sit in a chair like that, they'd put us in jail.

50

RUBY UPCHURCH, *ignoring her*: And look at that picture. She got herself flat as a piece of paper. And there you are, *to Ray Burgess*. Look there. Don't he look handsome standing there holding that cat? *Seeing him smile*: That cat goes with you. You can tell how much she loves you the way she's laying there on her back. Cats don't do that unless they trust you. Look at her. *Pauses*. Look at that Opal just laying there in Abraham's bosom. Look how she goes with that suit you got on. You're both the same color, kind of brown-gray I'd call it.

RAY BURGESS: MATCH.

RUBY UPCHURCH: MATCH? Ain't that clever? He bought a suit to go with his cat. Ain't that something? *She turns to Ray Burgess*: And it shows. The trouble you took. Anybody looking at that picture would say, 'That man looks just like that cat.' And then they'd stop and think a minute, and you know what they'd say? — *teasing*.

RAY BURGESS: WHAT?

RUBY UPCHURCH: They'd say, 'Or maybe that cat looks just like that man.' *She laughs*.

ORA BELLE IVEY: What happened to it?

RAY BURGESS, *looking at her while his hand speaks*: CANCER.

RUBY UPCHURCH: It died of cancer. Oh. *It is as though she has lost her breath*. You poor man. *She pauses*. My husband died of cancer. I remember standing beside the bed. He didn't even know I was there. He'd cry out and break my heart. The drugs couldn't touch it. I didn't want him to suffer, but I couldn't bear to let him go. *Pauses*. It felt like I'd lose him. *Pauses*. Then he died, and I felt better after that.

ORA BELLE IVEY: Of course you did. That's why he's buried, so you can forget him. Two weeks ago, wasn't it? It couldn't have been two weeks ago he died and was buried.

RUBY UPCHURCH, *angrily*: Fifty-eight days. It was fifty-eight days ago.

RAY BURGESS, *shifting his hand back and forth*: NO, NO.

ORA BELLE IVEY: *She waves at Ray Burgess as though to get him to stop distracting her. To Ruby Upchurch:* Are you sure? I could have sworn it was two weeks ago. *Without waiting for an answer she turns to Ray Burgess:* Stop that. I can't think of what I'm saying with you jiggling like that.

Ruby Upchurch stills his hand and remains beside him holding it.

ORA BELLE IVEY, *to Ray Burgess:* That's why we got her to come out with me. We figured she might not feel so sorry for herself if she got to see cases like you, laying in bed the rest of their life with a stroke, scrabbling words on some kind of board. And that's why we're here. This is the first time she's been out of the house in fifty-eight days. I mean on a social visit. They say her husband was awful sick, *confiding to Ray Burgess*. He died for months. Eat up with cancer.

RUBY UPCHURCH, *crying suddenly*: What's this? *pointing to the photograph album.* Look at that picture. Ever see a room like that? It's all beige and white.

ORA BELLE IVEY: Let me see, *shouldering Ruby Upchurch aside.* Beige and white. Must be hard to keep clean.

RUBY UPCHURCH: Look at that white rug. I never did see a white rug before.

ORA BELLE IVEY: Looks like a bedsheet. *To Ray Burgess*: How long your cat live?

Ray Burgess' finger stabs the number three and stops there, pointing.

ORA BELLE IVEY: Three years. That ain't very long. Most cats live longer than that unless they get hit by a car or somebody poisons them. Yours died quick.

RUBY UPCHURCH: Look there. Look at that baby.

ORA BELLE IVEY, *grabbing the album*: Let me see.

RUBY UPCHURCH: Don't she look pretty laying there on the rug by the fire.

ORA BELLE IVEY: Sure is clean.

RUBY UPCHURCH: And look there. It must be Christmas. Look at her smiling.

ORA BELLE IVEY, *smiling herself. It is clear she loves children:* I like how she's smiling. She got a smile on her face like she just woke up and said hello to herself in a mirror. Looks like somebody glued it on her.

RUBY UPCHURCH: Let's turn the page. *Surprised:* There she is again.

ORA BELLE IVEY: And look at her smiling. She's smiling at something she knows she ain't telling.

RUBY UPCHURCH: Who's that man?

ORA BELLE IVEY, *pushing her aside*: What man?

RUBY UPCHURCH: The one in the white shirt.

ORA BELLE IVEY: Sure is fat. Look at that stomach. Sticks out so far he got his shirt dirty in front rubbing on things. Look how he's staring. And look at that sweet child smiling again.

RUBY UPCHURCH: Ain't she pretty.

ORA BELLE IVEY: Got a nice smile. I always did like a smiler like that. She must have had a happy childhood. Makes me feel good just to see her looking so happy. There's time enough for grief later on when all the smiling dries up on your face like froth.

RUBY UPCHURCH: She grew up to be a pretty woman — *turning another page*.

RAY BURGESS: LISA.

RUBY UPCHURCH: LISA. I wish my name was Lisa. What a lovely name that is. *To Ora Belle Ivey*: Don't you wish you had a lovely name like Lisa?

ORA BELLE IVEY: No I don't. I always liked Ora Belle for a woman and Gilmer for a man. Gilmer was my daddy's name.

RUBY UPCHURCH: And Ora Belle was your momma's?

ORA BELLE IVEY: No. I was named for a maiden aunt, never would marry. It runs in the family. Lots of Iveys ain't interested in that. *Shyly*: Ora Belle means some kind of goddess.

RUBY UPCHURCH: Goddess?

ORA BELLE IVEY: One of them in some far-off land. The goddess of plenty. *Shyly*: My momma said,

'Be happy with it, Ora Belle. Your name means some kind of goddess of plenty.' That's why I try to be plentiful.

RUBY UPCHURCH, *to Ray Burgess*: Lisa married or she still lives with your wife, or what?

RAY BURGESS: ZIMMERMAN.

RUBY UPCHURCH: ZIMMERMAN? That's your wife's brother? *Then suddenly*: I see. The man in the picture with Lisa, the one in the white shirt. That's Zimmerman.

RAY BURGESS: YES. FATHER.

ORA BELLE IVEY: FATHER? He ain't your father.

RUBY UPCHURCH: He didn't mean that. He meant the man in the picture is Lisa's father. *To Ray Burgess*: Ain't that right?

RAY BURGESS: YES.

RUBY UPCHURCH: See there? *To Ray Burgess*: She ain't your daughter at all then, is she? I was wrong, wasn't I?

RAY BURGESS: MINE.

ORA BELLE IVEY: MINE? What you mean MINE? Sometimes I think I'm wasting my time coming down here. They can't talk. They can't hear. They can't spell. Sometimes I wonder. And then there'll be someone who comes up and says they sure are happy to see you and kiss your cheek and tell you how pretty you look. And you start to go, they say, 'Don't go.' 'I don't want you to leave me.' Well I tell you when I hear that, it makes it seem almost like it's worth it. *She turns back to Ray Burgess*: She ain't your baby if she's Zimmerman's baby in the picture.

RUBY UPCHURCH: He means he loved her like she was his.

RAY BURGESS: YES.

RUBY UPCHURCH: And you were their friend?

RAY BURGESS: MORE.

ORA BELLE IVEY: MORE? What's more? Stop lying. There's ain't no more unless you're some kind of kin or something.

RAY BURGESS: MORE, MORE.

RUBY UPCHURCH: MORE? You're more than a friend?

RAY BURGESS: LOVED.

RUBY UPCHURCH: LOVED. You loved them? You loved the Zimmermans?

RAY BURGESS: FAMILY.

RUBY UPCHURCH: FAMILY? They were your family? You lived with them, *suddenly understanding.* You lived in their house, and they were your family. You never married.

RAY BURGESS: YES.

RUBY UPCHURCH: And this was your family, and Lisa was like your little girl. How long did you live with them?

Ray Burgess' finger stabs the number 1 and then the number 6.

RUBY UPCHURCH: Sixteen years. You lived with them for sixteen years. What a long time. I was married forty-two years.

ORA BELLE IVEY, *shouting suspiciously*: You some kind of boarder, or what?

RAY BURGESS: YES. *And then*: LOVE.

RUBY UPCHURCH: LOVE. At first it may have been money, and then it was like your own family. You got to see Lisa grow up and love them and be with them.

RAY BURGESS: YES, YES.

RUBY UPCHURCH: Lisa must have loved you just like a daddy. Wasn't she lucky? She had you and Zimmerman both. She had two daddies.

ORA BELLE IVEY: One was enough for me. I loved my daddy. I wouldn't want another.

RAY BURGESS: OPAL.

RUBY UPCHURCH, *in quick sympathy*: OPAL. She loved you, too. Yes, she must have. That's why you put her first in the book. I knew you loved her as soon as I saw it.

ORA BELLE IVEY: That's why it's such a pity she died. Pets of all sorts are bad about dying. *To Ray Burgess*: Three years ain't no time. I bet you just got where you loved her, and then she was gone. That's the way it is with them pets. They're short livers.

RUBY UPCHURCH: Three years. What's three years? Or forty-two years, or three hundred and sixty-five years? They're all the same, all the years I ever lived. *Pause.* I can't even remember the sound of his voice. And then when he died, it was all over. I remember leaving him that first night and going home and getting in bed and thinking about him under the ground with all that dirt on him and how cold it is and what happens there, and I couldn't even cry out and call him. But ever since I been in this room, I feel like I'm supposed to be here, waiting for something. Something's coming.

ORA BELLE IVEY: I wouldn't doubt it. *To Ray Burgess*: What were you doing in Newark, New Jersey all by yourself? Why didn't you stay home? I was born and raised right here, and I stayed here with my momma and daddy.

RAY BURGESS: POOR.

RUBY UPCHURCH: He was poor. He needed a job.

ORA BELLE IVEY: So are lots of folks. Look at me. I was poor and needed ajob. But I helped myself. And now look at the difference. There you are laying there, and me standing here, come to visit. Newark, New Jersey's a sick place to work I hear. Lots of folks go to work there, come down with strokes and can't even move. Lay all day like my momma looking at a spot on the ceiling.

RAY BURGESS: ELECTRICIAN.

RUBY UPCHURCH: ELECTRICIAN? Look at that, He was an electrician. Ain't that a coincidence? My husband was an electrician. You love your work?

RAY BURGESS: YES.

RUBY UPCHURCH: That's what he said. He used to try to tell me about it. When he came to where he told me about light and how it came on, he squeezed my arm. *She touches Ray Burgess to illustrate.* He said

light, and his fingers contracted, and it was like light
in my arm, it was so fast — like a flash. We lived
together so long I knew what he meant before he even
knew it himself — *laughing*.

ORA BELLE IVEY: Folks don't know what other
folks thinking. That's my observation. What other folks
think's a mystery. You take my momma. When she got
like him—laying in bed waiting to die—ain't no telling
what she was thinking. She was laying there with her
eyes wide open staring at a spot on the ceiling. And I'd
say, 'Momma, momma. What're you thinking about,
staring at that spot all day? Don't you get tired? Things
like that, to cheer her up. I used to sit there and watch
her. It wasn't like him. Her mind was clear as a bell,
and she could talk if she wanted to. But she didn't
want to. Momma never did say a word, and I never
did figure out what she was thinking about, staring at
the ceiling like that. She died with the mystery still in
her mouth before she could figure it out, what it
meant.

RUBY UPCHURCH: What mystery?

ORA BELLE IVEY: What? Her whole life. *As though
speaking to herself*: Like when you drown, you see
your whole life flash before you, like a great light, and
there it is from beginning to end before you slip under
and die in the waves. After the funeral, I went up in
the room where she died, and I was alone. *Ruby
Upchurch gets up and walks toward Ora Belle Ivey.*
And the wind was blowing, and the house was
creaking, and I thought it was somebody coming up
the stairs creaking across the floor, and then it was
like it came in the room and I looked around and said,
Who's there? But nobody answered. And all of a
sudden it was like some kind of blessing in there, and I
heard this voice, said, 'Ora Belle, you weren't able to
help your momma. She died staring at a spot on the
ceiling, thinking something you don't even know what,

like she was somewhere in some far-off land. But what about the rest of them? There's lots of others dying right now, this very minute. Old folks home's full of them, dying right and left. What about them? And that's where I first got the idea of the errand of mercy. It's like somebody walked in the room and whispered it to me, except there wasn't nobody there. *During this speech Ruby Upchurch reaches out her hand and touches Ora Belle Ivey as though to comfort her. Ora Belle Ivey becomes aware of what is happening and pulls away abruptly, looking about her as though adjusting her eyes to an excess of light.* Well I swear — *as though surprised.* Listen to that. Will you just listen to that, how I was talking? I swear, you all must be good company to get me to talking like that. I'm usually the quiet type. My momma used to say, 'You're the quiet type, Ora Belle. That's why you ain't married.' But it wasn't that. *She falls silent again, glaring about her as though in anger.*

RAY BURGESS: I WANT OUT.

ORA BELLE IVEY, *shouting*: You see that?

RUBY UPCHURCH, *crying*: What, what?

ORA BELLE IVEY: Look it there — *pointing at Ray Burgess.*

RAY BURGESS: I WANT OUT.

ORA BELLE IVEY: Look at that. Ain't that awful? All they want to do is die.

RUBY UPCHURCH: Die? He didn't say he wanted to die.

ORA BELLE IVEY: He said he wants out. What you think that means? That means dying.

RUBY UPCHURCH: No. No. No. He can't die. He wants to live. He wants to get well and get out of here and go back to Newark, New Jersey, and take up his old job he loves so much and get him a new cat he can call Ruby.

ORA BELLE IVEY: That's your name.

RUBY UPCHURCH, *correcting herself*: Or Ora Belle. That's a lovely name for a cat. Ora Belle. Don't it sound rich? That's a plentiful name for a cat.

ORA BELLE IVEY: That's because it's named for the goddess of plenty.

RUBY UPCHURCH, *to Ray Burgess*: Wouldn't you just love a new cat in Newark, New Jersey? You could call it Ruby or Ora Belle, the goddess of plenty.

Ray Burgess looks at her.

RUBY UPCHURCH: A tiger cat, a grey and striped tiger. Then you get you a sport coat. My husband has one. I got it at home — black and grey tweed. Match that cat perfect. And you could get dressed up on Sunday and ride to church with the Zimmermans . . .

ORA BELLE IVEY: They're all Jews.

RUBY UPCHURCH: They ain't Jews. They all go to church every Sunday. George and Rose and Lisa and her husband and babies. They're all Methodists and get in the car and go to the Methodist church all together.

RAY BURGESS: DEAD.

ORA BELLE IVEY: DEAD? You see that DEAD?

RUBY UPCHURCH, *ignoring her*: What you mean,

DEAD?

RAY BURGESS: ZIMMERMANS.

RUBY UPCHURCH: The Zimmermans are dead? All the Zimmermans? They are all dead? I don't believe it. *She rushes to the bed and opens the photograph album, jamming her finger at it. Ora Belle Ivey pushes her aside to look.* There they are. Look at them laughing. Look at them standing here hugging each other. Look at that grass. That grass is green.

ORA BELLE IVEY: Look at that smile. She's still smiling.

RUBY UPCHURCH: And that dress. That dress is bright and fresh as the day I first married. They can't be dead. They still got their hair. Their eyes ain't sunk in the back of their heads. They know where they are. Look at that living room. See that white rug? That's where they're supposed to be, and they don't ever want to leave. *Breaking down.* What happened to them? What could have happened?

RAY BURGESS: AUTO.

RUBY UPCHURCH: AUTO.

ORA BELLE IVEY, *patting his arm*: There, there. Don't cry. You're too old and sick to be crying. Besides which, think of God's mercy. Auto accidents are fast. You get in one of them, you're dead before you even know it. One minute you're saying, Hold on, Hold on there, and the next minute you're laying on the pavement bleeding from the side of the mouth where your head's crushed in by the door knob in the back. And I say, Thank God. Thank God for that. Better that than what he got, watching TV and getting bedsores.

RUBY UPCHURCH, *touching Ray Burgess*: Oh, you

poor man.

ORA BELLE IVEY: He still got that photograph album.

RUBY UPCHURCH: A piece of lawn, somebody smiling at herself — *breaking off*. Lisa died too? *It is more a statement than a question, a cry of the heart.*

ORA BELLE IVEY: Of course she did. All them Zimmermans died at once. All in the same car on the highway. You heard what he said.

RAY BURGESS: LISA ALIVE.

RUBY UPCHURCH: Alive? Oh thank God.

RAY BURGESS: ALIVE CA.

RUBY UPCHURCH, *suddenly understanding*: ALIVE CA. Lisa Zimmerman's alive in California. O thank God. It's like Lazarus come back from the dead, and they pick the worms off him, and see who it is . . . It seems like some kind of miracle. *To Ray Burgess*: I'm so happy. *Kisses him.*

ORA BELLE IVEY, *suspiciously*: She married or what? How she get out to California?

RAY BURGESS: NO, NO.

ORA BELLE IVEY, *looking at his hand moving back and forth as she would at something singularly distasteful. To Ruby Upchurch, indicating Ray Burgess' continued negation*: Whatever that means. Maybe you know. *She pauses.* Let's go. Time to go. We're wasting our time. There's many another needs cheering up. This ain't the only one in the poor house. Think of the others laying there waiting to kiss our hands and thank us for coming. *To Ray Burgess*: And quit that scribble scrabble. Nobody likes to see that scribble scrabble, guess what I'm saying. That's distracting. It gets in the way of cheering you up.

RUBY UPCHURCH, *to Ray Burgess*: Why don't Lisa come and get you? She could take you home to California.

RAY BURGESS: NO.

RUBY UPCHURCH: No? You're like her daddy. She'd love to have you. I can tell by the way she smiles. A smile like that — got self-possession. *Pausing*: She loves you don't she?

RAY BURGESS: DEAD.

ORA BELLE IVEY: DEAD? Let's go. See there, *indicating Ray Burgess*. It's time to go. He gets talking like that.

RUBY UPCHURCH, *crying in discovery*: I know. She's alive, but she don't want you. She don't love you. She loves herself. I can see how she smiles at herself — like in a mirror.

ORA BELLE IVEY, *shouting, moving toward the bed and patting Ray Burgess' shoulder*: There, there. Don't cry. Ain't no need to get upset about somebody in California may not even be alive. It's all mixed up. She's dead, she's alive — who knows what it all means. But it don't matter, *turning back to Ray Burgess*. Don't worry about it. You still got us standing right here beside you on an errand of mercy ready to fetch whatever you want or call somebody to get it for you, if we're too dressed to do it ourselves. Here hold my hand. *She reaches over to the edge of the bed as into the zone of another dimension. She grasps his free hand, pinning it in hers. Assuming a professional manner*: How are you feeling? You eating good? *Ruby*

Upchurch watches while Ora Belle Ivey grasps the ouija board with her free hand and wrenches it loose from Ray Burgess. There. She has a firm grip on it and draws it to her. That's better. To Ruby Upchurch: He won't get so upset. The way he has to talk he gets tired.

RUBY UPCHURCH, *ignoring Ora Belle Ivey, following her own line of thought:* Listen. I feel like my feet have gone to sleep all over my body, and I been walking on stumps of wood where I couldn't feel them, and now the blood's coming back. It's prickling like needles. Like in that game. You ever play it when you were a child? *To Ora Belle Ivey:* Give me your hand.

ORA BELLE IVEY, *suspiciously:* What for? Use his, *indicating Ray Burgess.*

RUBY UPCHURCH: Hold it up like this. *Ora Belle Ivey holds up her hand.* Not that. The other one. Get them to match. *They place their hands palm to palm.* Now take your other hand and rub it up and down on it like this. *Ora Belle Ivey reaches out and slides her hand up and down, then flings it away as though it is on fire.*

ORA BELLE IVEY: O God. Don't touch me. That's awful.

RUBY UPCHURCH: What's it feel like?

ORA BELLE IVEY: I ain't saying.

RUBY UPCHURCH: What's it remind you of?

ORA BELLE IVEY: I ain't saying.

RUBY UPCHURCH: What?

ORA BELLE IVEY: A finger.

RUBY UPCHURCH: A dead man's finger. You can't even tell whose it is. It don't feel like yours. That's what I mean. *Pauses.* I was like that all over. And now now all of a sudden the blood's coming back. You know that story about your momma and how you heard the house creaking and you thought it was her coming back?

ORA BELLE IVEY: Of couse I do. Who you think you heard it from — him? — *indicating Ray Burgess.*

RUBY UPCHURCH, *ignoring her*: As soon as I came in this room I heard the footsteps on the stairs.

ORA BELLE IVEY: What stairs?

RUBY UPCHURCH: The stairs of my heart. And I said to myself, Here it comes. I hear it creaking. I could feel it coming closer, and then it was in the room with me. I could almost reach out and touch it. I kept waiting for it to speak. I figured it was some kind of message. It was so close. It was like something I almost forgot on the tip of my tongue. Except it wasn't words.

ORA BELLE IVEY: It wasn't words with me either.

RUBY UPCHURCH: It's like he reached out and touched me, put his hand on me and touched me, and there are no words, only mercy. I feel flooded with infinite mercy. And I say, Thank God. Thank God Ray Burgess. Thank God you're alive. Thank God, thank God Ora Belle Ivey. Thank God Lisa Zimmerman. Thank God you ain't dead in that accident. Thank God I still love him. *Breaking off:* I got so much mercy. I got infinite mercy. It died and was buried, and now it's come back.

ORA BELLE IVEY: And that's all?

RUBY UPCHURCH: Yes.

ORA BELLE IVEY: Then in that case, that ain't it. That ain't the same thing at all. Something happened to me. I felt this kind of infinite mercy, and it changed my whole life. It changed my whole life. I ain't like I was. *She glares about triumphantly, like the Antichrist, then picks up the thread of her life again.* You ready? We got to go. Errands of mercy don't last forever. There're too many needy crying out for teeth and eyeglasses, not to mention cheering them up, giving them something to think about besides being old and dying of cancer unless they're too far gone to know it, in which case we generally give them some candy. That makes them happy. *Ruby Upchurch pushes past Ora Belle Ivey and stands beside Ray Burgess.*

RUBY UPCHURCH: Don't go. *She touches his arm.*

ORA BELLE IVEY, *to Ruby Upchurch*: Don't cry. You look like my momma.

RUBY UPCHURCH, *ecstatic*: I ain't crying. It's because I'm so happy. I'm crying because of that infinite mercy.

ORA BELLE IVEY: My momma cried like that all day at the end, and I couldn't stop her. That's why I can't stand it.

RUBY UPCHURCH: I ain't crying. *To Ray Burgess*: Stay here with me. No need to go to California. I got a big house, needs rewiring.

ORA BELLE IVEY: Might as well. That Lisa out there's dead already. She don't want you. *She looks down and sees she is still holding the ouija board. It is like discovering she has absentmindedly picked up a piece of dried dog turd. She thrusts it from her. To*

Ruby Upchurch: Here. Ruby Upchurch is too far away to give it to, so Ora Belle Ivey puts it down on the foot of the bed. Ruby Upchurch walks toward her, picks it up, and starts to give it back to Ray Burgess when she notices he is still holding the photograph album. She takes the album from him.

RUBY UPCHURCH: Here, you won't need this. I'll put it over here. *She lifts the blue towel on the chair and puts the album back under it.*

ORA BELLE IVEY: All them old times are gone. You hear that? Listen to me. Get out your glasses and read the paper. That'll give you something of interest to do. There're lots of good times in that, you get reading the paper and quit staring up at the ceiling. *To Ruby Upchurch*: You reckon he can read?

RUBY UPCHURCH: Why don't you ask him? *She hands Ray Burgess back the ouija board. He takes it from her and slips it under the covers.*

ORA BELLE IVEY: Him? *She examines Ray Burgess.* He can work that board. But he can't talk. It's like hash in there — *tapping his head. She pauses.* He can't read. We're wasting our time. Let's go. Here — *turning to Ray Burgess.* Here's you some candy. Suck on that. *She takes a peppermint candy cane from her purse, the kind made for Christmas. To Ruby Upchurch, passing it to her*: Here, give him this. That'll keep him busy till we come back.

Ruby Upchurch gives Ray Burgess the candy cane and squeezes his arm and pats his shoulder.

RUBY UPCHURCH, *to Ray Burgess*: I'm coming back. I'm coming back every day.

ORA BELLE IVEY: So am I. Wild horses couldn't keep me, not if they tied me to them. I'd drag them after to get to this room.

RUBY UPCHURCH, *to Ray Burgess*: So would I.

ORA BELLE IVEY: Who wouldn't? Let's go. *She pushes out into the hallway.* Suck on that candy till you get your teeth, *she calls back over her shoulder.* Cut that light off, *she shouts to Ruby Upchurch, who is just leaving the room. Ruby Upchurch cuts off the light. Total darkness.*

PRIOR
ENGAGEMENTS

Prior Engagements was first produced by Theater Emory at the Atlanta New Play Project in June 1985 and later at Emory University in the fall of 1985. It was directed by James W. Flannery. The set and lighting were designed by Randy Fullerton. The production manager was Robert Schultz, and the cast consisted of Suzi Bass, Jill Jane Clements, Andy Cole, Pat Hurley, John Purcell, and Andre Wiggins.

The Baptism of Water and *The Call of Nature* were produced in December 1986 at the Victory Gardens Studio Theatre, Chicago, Illinois, under the title of *Prior Engagements*. The play was directed by Dennis Zacek, Artistic Director. The cast consisted of P. J. Brown, Anne Bernadette Coyle, Paul Gilmartin, Ed Hofmann, Toni Potts, and Christopher Williams. The sets were designed by James Dardenne, the lighting by Maureen Kennedy, and the costumes by Ellen E. Jones.

The Baptism of Water

SCENE

401 Adams Street, Decatur, Georgia

CAST OF CHARACTERS

THE NARRATOR
THE WOMAN
THE MAN
THE POLICEMAN

Moonlight.

A woman is discovered sleeping. Nearby in the yard is a large outdoor water faucet. It is as big around as a small bore cannon.

As the woman sleeps, a figure enters, either a man or a woman — it does not matter which — dressed in white. It acknowledges the audience, then walks into the house. This is the character referred to in the stage directions as the Narrator. In the play itself the role is never precisely defined. At times it seems like an aspect of the play, at other times a function of the audience. It knows the woman's thoughts, but it also stands apart from them. It is both a form of mentalized reality and something beyond that — some other dimension of time and space that manifests itself in our lives. It is from this the play emerges, and it is toward this the play proceeds.

Inside the house the figure stands beside the sleeping woman, looking down at her. Then it turns to the audience and speaks.

NARRATOR: She stirs in her sleep and dreams of the first time she saw the ocean. It was in Florida. She and her husband travelled three days on bad roads in

a borrowed car to top the dune and cut off the engine
and look. It was moving. That was the first thing she
noticed. It was like some kind of animal breathing. It
moved toward them and then moved back like the gills
of a fish opening and closing. At the edge was a dribble
of seaweed and trash, and the beach itself was littered
with boards and cow shit. In the distance were the
cows, moving ahead of them as though herded. They
drove up the beach on the hard sand beside the ocean.
It heaved on itself as though swelling with passion.
She kept her eyes on the cows, and when they turned
off into the shrub, she insisted that they turn off and
follow them. The cows kept looking back and trotting,
and her husband kept saying they were going to end
up in Mexico. The only way them cows are going is
away from this car. But she was looking for the
highway and when they found it insisted they keep on
going until they got back to Georgia. It was to have
been their honeymoon. The year was 1948.

*As the narration continues, a man enters the yard.
He wanders about the stage like an apparition,
eventually discovering the water faucet and turning it
on just as the Narrator describes the woman's dream.
It is difficult to tell if this is a reenactment of the
dream or an actual happening.*

NARRATOR: She stirs again, rolling over on her left
side. Her feet are sticking out from under the covers.
They are so white in the moonlight they look artificial,
the toes running up them like scars. She pulls them
back inside the covers. The motion is slow and
hydraulic. They disappear just about the same time
she dreams that it is still last winter when the faucet
outside her window ran for an hour before she got up
and saw the driveway was covered with ice. She
thought then of the ocean. The ice in the driceway was
like the still part in the distance where it came to end
at the sky. Then she thought of God. Nothing moved
except the water turning to ice. It was filling the world

with silence. Something had come that filled her with fear, and here it had happened again. She is awake now. Someone has come and turned on the faucet again.

The woman gets out of bed and goes to the window. She sees the man in the yard standing beside the faucit. The water is turned on so hard it splaches in all directions at once like a fountain.

NARRATOR: The water looks silver. It flashes through the air like knives. She surprises herself by thinking how beautiful it is. And then she thinks of the violation. It's not only wasting her water and flooding the yard and costing her money, it's using her things however he wants to.

She raps on the window. The man does not look up. She raps until her knuckles hurt, but she still cannot get his attention. She opens the window.

NARRATOR: The night air fills her with rapture. She thinks of ghosts manifesting themselves in pools of cold air. It is like that, only more lovely.

WOMAN: What are you doing? *The man is a few feet below her.* Turn off that water.

The man looks around as though searching for a voice. He keeps looking up, towards the roofs of the houses or the tops of the trees, trying to locate it.

WOMAN: I said turn it off.

The man just stands there.

WOMAN: You hear me?

MAN: Not until you let me in.

WOMAN: Let you in? *She is truly surprised.* Turn off that water.

In the silence that follows the man seems to notice that his leg is getting wet. He shakes it like a dog and moves a foot or so away so that most of the water falls on his shoe. The man lifts the foot that is getting wet and stomps it. He keeps stomping it.

WOMAN: Stop that. You're ruining my lawn. Get out of here.

MAN: Not until you let me in.

WOMAN: Let you in? I'm not fixing to let you in. Get away. I'm calling the police. Turn off that water.

NARRATOR: The man is still stomping his foot. She takes her robe from the foot of the bed and is out of the house and across to the faucet before the man even knows she has come. She turns off the water.

WOMAN: Now leave it off, or I'm going to have to call the police.

She goes in the house and gets back into bed.

NARRATOR: It's like a dream — the sudden inexplicable apparition, the odd detail like the running water, the faucet turned on for no good reason, someone wanting to get into the house — and she remembers once when she was a girl . . .

WOMAN: A woman appeared and rang the doorbell. She had come in a taxi, and as soon as I had opened the door she pushed past me into the living room. My mother stood up as the woman sat down and said, Who are you? and the woman waved at her as though she were deaf and dumb. She's drunk, my mother said. How'd she get in here? We found an address in the woman's bag and got a taxi and took her home. Her husband accepted her at the door like a package sent to the wrong address.

Suddenly the door bell rings, and the woman leaps as though at the cry of a baby. It keeps on ringing every four seconds. At first it is annoying. Then disturbing.

WOMAN: What right does he have to do this to me?

She gets out of bed and goes to the door. She puts her mouth to the crack.

WOMAN: Quit that. Quit ringing that door bell. Get out of here.

MAN: I turned off the water.

WOMAN: You turned off the water? What a liar. I could never tolerate a liar. I turned off that water. Don't lie about it. You crazy or what?

Long pause.

MAN: Let me in.

WOMAN: Get out of here. I already told you. I'm not fixing to let you in.

The man rings the door bell again. He keeps on ringing it at four second intervals.

WOMAN: Listen to me, you're disturbing my rest. This is my house you're breaking and entering. That's my water you spilled on the ground. That's my door bell. You're wearing it out. Electric and water cost me money. I'm not fixing to let you in.

The doorbell stops.

MAN: Why not?

WOMEN: Why not? *The question is so unexpected she hardly knows where to begin.* Because you don't deserve to be let in, that's why. Because you might rape me, then cut me up in little pieces and flush me down the toilet, and the sewer gets stopped up, and you have to call the plumber, and he comes and smells human flesh, and they get you for murder, but that doesn't matter, I'm dead anyway.

NARRATOR: She is thinking about the story of a mass murder she heard on the evening news.

WOMAN: Let you in? *The outrage returns.* Why should I let you in?

NARRATOR: As soon as she says it, she knows there's no reason why she should let him in.

MAN: Because I live here.

The woman is stunned. She steps back from the door and inspects it. Just then the door bell rings, and she rushes to the crack and cries into it.

WOMAN: I'm calling the police. If you aren't out of here in three seconds, I'm calling the police, and don't think I won't do it. I called the police on better than you are many a time. They know where I live. They don't even ask my address.

The door in front of her is silent. She looks at it as though it might explode any minute. Then she tiptoes across the room to the window that looks out on the porch. She draws the curtain aside so stealthily it never moves. She puts her eye to it and sees the man leaning against the screen door. He is bending over taking off his pants. He removes one leg, then loses his balance. Then he has them off, and the belt buckle clatters on the floor. The sound startles her, and she rushes to the phone, then hesitates and returns to the window.

She watches as the man unbuttons his shirt. Then he removes his socks, then his shirt, then his jockey shorts. Then he walks across the yard to the water faucet and turns it on.

WOMAN: What are you doing?

MAN: Taking a shower.

WOMAN: Turn off that water. I'm calling the police.

A second later he turns off the water. She stands there and waits.

MAN: Let me in.

He pounds on the wall and scratches at the door like a dog.

WOMAN: Get your clothes on — *speaking into the crack at the door.* Aren't you ashamed of yourself looking like that.

MAN. Like what?

WOMAN: Like you look.

MAN: I can't help it.

WOMAN: Then cover it up. That's what I do.

MAN: I'm getting tired.

WOMAN: You're getting tired. What is that, some kind of joke? It's 2:30 in the morning, and you're getting tired? What do you think I'm doing?

MAN: Keeping me up. If it wasn't for you I'd be in bed.

WOMAN: Whose bed? That's what I mean. You stay right there.

MAN: What for?

WOMAN: I'm calling the police. You haven't got enough sense to keep your clothes on, I want them to see it. Stay right there. They're going to think that's something, they see you looking streaked like that.

MAN: Streaked?

WOMAN: All that hair. Looks streaked.

NARRATOR: In the moonlight the surface of his skin is striped. The hair swirls across him in patterns like animal markings.

WOMAN: They see that, they say what is it — man or beast?

MAN: Man.

WOMAN: I know that — *perceiving his interest.* — But they don't. You want them to see you looking like that?

Long pause. Then something crashes against the door. The woman runs to the window and looks out. The man is trying to put his shirt on his legs. She raps on the window.

WOMAN: That's your shirt. You're trying to put it on your legs. You getting dressed?

MAN: I was, but I'm too tired. Let me in. I got to get to work in the morning.

WOMAN: Work?

NARRATOR: She can not conceive of him as a person. He is like something from the sea or something webbed that fell from the sky.

WOMAN: He's trying to rape me. That's why he took off his clothes. If I let him in, he'll turn in a minute.

MAN: Thanks for the shower.

She rushes to the window. The porch is empty. She runs back to the door and puts her mouth against the crack.

WOMAN: Where are you? You go or what? O Dear God, don't let him go. How are the police going to know where he's at? *To the man:* You want a cookie? You like candy?

MAN: No ma'am. *His mouth is right beside hers at the door. She can almost feel his breath.* You got a marijuana cigarette?

WOMAN: A marijuana cigarette? Of course not. What would I do with a marijuana cigarette?

MAN: Give it to me.

WOMAN: I got more things to do with my time than stand here at 2:30 in the morning and give out marijuana cigarettes.

MAN: You got any candy?

WOMAN: Of course I got candy. *She is just as surprised as when he asked for a marijuana cigarette.* I got candy all over the house. I got peppermints and caramel, Indian corn and Hershey kisses. What kind you like?

But he is not there. Something has withdrawn. The connection is lost.

WOMAN: What's your name? What do they call you? You there?

She runs to the window and looks out. He is not there. Then she sees the pile of clothes in the front of the door.

WOMAN: Thank God for that anyway. He left his clothes. Even the shoes. He can't get far without his shoes. *She runs to the phone, gets out the book, and dials the number.*

NARRATOR: Police — *accenting the first syllable.* You got some business? *The voice is firm. It does not have time to waste.*

WOMAN: I want to report a drug fiend. He's high on something, asking for drugs, and I told him I just smoke cigarettes. That's drugs enough at my time of life.

NARRATOR: You got something to report?

WOMAN: Of course I have. That's what I'm trying to tell you about. *She is suddenly angry.* You think I'd call you up just to talk? *She hangs up.*

The woman stares at the phone in her hand, stunned at what she has done. Then she runs to the window. The man is sitting on the bannister putting on a shoe.

WOMAN: Stop that. *She raps at the window.*

The man swings his head up like a horse lifting it from a sack of feed. He is distracted but not very interested.

WOMAN: Stop that putting on your shoe. I just called the police. They say stay where you are, don't do anything, they'll be here in a minute. *She runs to the phone.* Hello, I want to report an accident. *She speaks before the operator has a chance to say Police.*

NARRATOR: What? What you say? *The conversation seems to be over before she realizes it had begun.*

WOMAN: I want to report an accident — *trying to disguise her voice.* We didn't touch anything.

NARRATOR: Name?

WOMAN: I don't know. *Pauses.* Wilbur Roach.

NARRATOR: Address?

WOMAN: I mean his name is Wilbur Roach. He's outside. I wouldn't let him in because he's naked.

NARRATOR: Why is he naked? — *suddenly interested.*

WOMAN: That's the accident.

NARRATOR: Address? *She speaks with the same indifference as before.*

WOMAN: 401 Adams Street. You know how to get here?

NARRATOR: Yes. Telephone number?

WOMAN: 377-7589.

NARRATOR: You need an ambulance?

WOMAN: It's not that kind of accident. Much obliged. *She hangs up.*

She tiptoes to the window and peeks out. The man has on his shoes and trousers. The socks are a puzzle. He has them in his hand and is inspecting them.

WOMAN: What's your name?

MAN: Wilbur Roach.

The woman looks behind her. The action is quick, spontaneous, almost a reflex. It is as though she expects to see someone there.

WOMAN: How you know that?

MAN: What?

WOMAN: Your name?

MAN: My name?

WOMAN: I just made it up.

MAN: What accident?

WOMAN: O thank God. He overheard me. *To the man:* Those are socks — *tapping on the glass so he will be sure to know what she is talking about.*

NARRATOR: She figures if he knew they were socks, he would have to take his shoes off and then put his socks on and then the shoes, and by that time the police would be there.

The man puts the socks on the toe of each shoe and walks toward her across the porch. He puts his face to hers at the window.

MAN: Let me in. I live here.

NARRATOR: She can't bear to look at him. He is too

homeless, too forlorn. She looks at the face outside the window. It is like a baby left on her doorstep. She will never let it in.

The man turns and walks across the porch and starts ringing the door bell.

WOMAN: As long as he's ringing I know where he's at.

The room suddenly fills with blue light like the inside of an icebox. There is a brief blast of a siren. She runs to the window. Someone is shining a flashlight onto the porch. It picks up the man and moves up and down him, and the man accepts it as though knowing he is the one it has come for. Then the light searches the house. It finally picks her out at the window, and she shields her eyes, then runs to the door and flings it open.

WOMAN: Over here, Officer.

The man turns and steps forward.

The woman screams. She slams the door in his face.

POLICEMAN, *rushing up*: Good God, what happened?

The man turns to look at the policeman as though he had already forgotten he was there. The policeman's face is thin and edged like a hatchet. It is mostly all moustache. He is neither black nor white, the usual categories, but some sort of foreigner.

The woman suddenly pushes the man in the small of the back. He jumps forward at the policeman.

POLICEMAN, *to the man*: Goddam, you almost got killed — *drawing his gun*. What do you think you're doing?

MAN: I live here.

WOMAN: He doesn't live here. That's the whole reason I called you. He's trying to get in. I don't know why. He's some kind of dope fiend.

The policeman draws the man aside and questions him briefly.

POLICEMAN, *lifting his voice*: You want to register a complaint?

WOMAN: He was naked. I was so scared. You going to arrest him?

POLICEMAN: He says he lives here.

WOMAN: And I say he doesn't. It's my house.

POLICEMAN: He says you're the landlady. He says he was taking a shower, how come he was naked.

WOMAN: Taking a shower. You know where he was taking a shower?

Before she can explain what happened, the man turns and walks away.

POLICEMAN: Hey Buddy . . .

The policeman goes after him. The woman unlatches the screen door and follows.

WOMAN, *shouting*: That's how he does.

She is standing on top of the steps looking down at them in the yard. The policeman jerks the man around and draws his hands behind his back. He is

*fumbling with them. It looks like a Red Cross
illustration of the Heimlich maneuver or some new
rescue technique.*

WOMAN: That's how he's been doing all night.
Coming and going and acting crazy. He's out of his
mind.

POLICEMAN, *breathing heavily*: I'm going to book
him. Son of a bitch resisting arrest.

*They are still clinging together. Then the policeman
pushes him away as though they had done something
together, some brutal act, and now they were finished
and he loathes himself for doing it. The man's arms
are still twisted behind his back.*

WOMAN: That's good. You got him handcuffed.
Where's your partner?

POLICEMAN: Partner? You got to be kidding.

WOMAN: I thought you had partners. One gets shot,
the other one's always there to protect him.

POLICEMAN: You're thinking of TV. We got short
staff. We got politicians, that's what we got. Politicians
for mayor, politicians for chief of police. What do you
expect? They going to protect you? *He sounds
angry.*

WOMAN: Who's going to protect *you*? That's what I
mean.

POLICEMAN: Me? I'm the policeman.

WOMAN, *smiling*: He might kill us both.

NARRATOR: She is enjoying the conversation. He
seems like such a nice young man even if he talks like

a Yankee and looks like one too.

WOMAN: You must be a brave young man . . . .

The policeman is groveling about the man's feet doing something, patting his shoes or tying the laces.

WOMAN: What are you doing?

The policeman does not answer. He begins feeling the man's legs. The man starts to walk away like a cow or horse undergoing some sort of treatment, not knowing what its master intends. The policeman tries to follow squatting, still patting the legs.

WOMAN: You might have to tie him up. He doesn't look like he's standing still.

The policeman rises and jerks the man's arms.

POLICEMAN: Goddam it, stay there. You're under search.

The man stands there like a horse. If it had been raining, the steam would have risen from his clothes.

WOMAN: At least he does what you tell him to . . . .

NARRATOR: She stops short, seeing the man look at her. He looks so lonely and forlorn, standing there waiting. It is like sadness or grief. She looked back on life, and it was all superficial, like lights on the ocean. The other moved beneath the surface like a great fish. Her mind was the sea in which it swam. The great hulk slid past, moving in her mind like a shadow.

WOMAN: I figured he might hurt himself.

POLICEMAN: Son of a bitch going to get hurt, he doesn't stand still.

WOMAN: I mean with him crazy. He might have something happen.

POLICEMAN: He already did.

WOMAN: I mean something bad. He might hurt himself. That's why I called you. When I saw him naked, I figured there wasn't no telling what might happen to him looking like that. He might come to some harm. I wanted to save him.

POLICEMAN: Look at him. Looks harmless, don't he? I seen them look like that, and they kick your nuts out. Excuse me, lady.

WOMAN, *ignoring him*: He might have set himself on fire. He wouldn't know what he was doing. Or fall down a manhole. I couldn't trust him. That's why I called, to get him protection. At least you wouldn't rob him and beat him. At least you're going to take care of him, see he doesn't harm himself until you find out what's the matter.

POLICEMAN: What's the matter?

WOMAN: If he's drunk or crazy.

The woman suddenly sees something out of the corner of her eye beside the bannister — a piece of white cloth, circular, indefinite.

WOMAN: He left his socks.

The policeman does not answer.

WOMAN: I said his socks are still on the porch.

POLICEMAN: He don't need them.

WOMAN: I don't want them on my porch.

POLICEMAN: Yes, ma'am. *He takes the man by the arm as though preparing to leave. The sound of a siren rises and falls coming toward them, proceeding hysterically in surges, the red light flashing.*

WOMAN: I said get his things off my porch. I don't want to have to see them.

The policeman stops and turns. He comes back and bends over the socks as though inspecting something dead.

WOMAN: You want a stick?

NARRATOR: The policeman looks at her, but does not reply. She senses something move, a flurry of white like a flock of birds, a blur on her right, and turns to see the man begin running. He rolls and waddles like a duck, hands clasped behind his back.

POLICEMAN: Let him go. He can't get far with them on his hands.

WOMAN, *crying*: He's not running on his hands.

NARRATOR: She thinks he might get loose and come back. She imagines him turning on the faucet and calling her name until she wakes from sleep and goes to the window and sees him standing there in the yard like a nightmare or whatever it is. She is not certain what to call it: a visitation of some sort, a call.

WOMAN, *shouting*: Go get him.

The policeman moves past her down the steps. The siren comes closer and begins to slow down. The wailing turns into a mechanical moan, loosing its fine edge of hysteria.

POLICEMAN, *turning*: You call an ambulance?

WOMAN, *shouting*: I can't remember. I think so. I told them it was an accident. They asked if I needed an ambulance. And I said I thought he might need a doctor. He might have been hurt.

The policeman turns, takes a few steps, and stops. He takes out his revolver and braces himself.

POLICEMAN: Stop. Stop or I'll shoot. *over his shoulder:* Son of a bitch, lady.

WOMAN, *shouting*: O my God. O my God.

The policeman fires off two rounds in rapid succession.

WOMAN, *shouting*: O my God, what happened?

NARRATOR: The policeman seems to be saying something. He turns and gestures. The sound is indistinct. Then he is running again. The lights of the ambulance are still coming. Then they stop. The siren is silent, and she knows he is dead.

WOMAN: Before they even open the door to ask what happened, I already knew he was dead.

The woman makes her way slowly back into the house, takes off her robe, arranges the pillows and lies down in bed.

NARRATOR: Toward morning, after they had taken her statement and gone, she lies in bed waiting for sleep. It never comes and she imagines herself lying there the rest of her life, night after night, waiting for sleep, her eyes open in the dark thinking. It is like looking out at the ocean. Nothing is there. She thinks about God and how it was a policeman that killed him and what he was doing there and who sent him.

WOMAN: I don't want to have anything to do with him the rest of my life if that's how it is. I'd just as soon stay here and never move, never get up, just lay here and stare at the ceiling if that's what it takes. I may not sleep, but I'm not going to think about it.

NARRATOR: She reads until her eyes tire. Then she turns off the light and props herself up on the pillows.

As the narration continues, the man enters the yard once again. He goes directly to the water faucet.

NARRATOR: It is like looking down a well. At the bottom there is a glint of something or other, flashing and bright. At first she thinks it is the reflection of her own face. Then she drops a rock and hears the faint sound of water cast back with the echo.

The man turns on the faucet.

NARRATOR: Without knowing, she has drifted off to sleep, head lolling on the pillows, and she hears the sound of water running. It is rising everywhere. It has already taken the street, and the cars are gone. The yard is gone, the driveway, the walk. It covers the steps, the foundation plantings. It has risen over the porch and seeps under the threshold like blood. She waits for what she knows will come next. The man had been sent by God. Soon she will get up and let him in.

He walks slowly toward the house.

Gradual darkness.

In the darkness is heard the sound of water.

The doorbell rings. It keeps on ringing.

PART TWO

Chickamauga

SCENE

The interior of the National Park Service Museum at the Chickamauga National Battlefield, Chickamauga, Georgia.

CAST OF CHARACTERS

VENTRIS TIDWELL, visitor
SONNY HIGHTOWER, visitor

Martial music

The stage lights come on to reveal two large blow-ups at the back of the stage, one of a young man in a Confederate uniform, the other a field full of dead soldiers. The remainder of the stage is bare except for an oak display case resembling a coffin. The room is bright with sunlight. The overall impression is one of clarity, cleanliness, and order.

Ventris Tidwell enters. He walks around the room a while studying various imaginary displays. A short while later Sonny Hightower enters. Ventris Tidwell glances at him. They consciously avoid one another the same way strangers in cities ignore one another by pretending they do not exist. Ventris Tidwell stops facing the audience. He looks out over their heads, studying an imaginary map. Sonny Hightower circles the room, then comes up and stands directly behind him. It looks like a game or comic routine, as though he is trying to hide or jump out and surprise him. He is close enough to breathe on the back of his neck. Ventris Tidwell does not seem to know he is there. They stand there a few minutes, image and after-image, substance and shodow.

SONNY HIGHTOWER: The blue ones say, 'Go' and

the red ones say, 'Stop.'

VENTRIS TIDWELL, *surprised:* What blue ones?

SONNY HIGHTOWER: The blue ones and the red ones — *gesturing.*

Long pause.

SONNY HIGHTOWER, *gesturing toward the map and smiling:* Fucking arrows.

VENTRIS TIDWELL: What? Don't talk like that. I don't like to hear talk like that. I heard too much of that in the army.

SONNY HIGHTOWER: Shit yeah.

VENTRIS TIDWELL: This is peacetime.

SONNY HIGHTOWER: Shit yeah.

Long pause. They study the map together.

VENTRIS TIDWELL: What's that you got on? You got on some kind of perfume or what? That some kind of after shave?

SONNY HIGHTOWER: Hell no. Perfume.

VENTRIS TIDWELL: Perfume? *He can't believe it.* Goddamn, that's what I thought. What are you, French or something?

SONNY HIGHTOWER: I'm American.

VENTRIS TIDWELL: Hell I know that. So am I. So's my whole family. We're all American. What I mean is what else are you? If you're American, you're something else besides American.

SONNY HIGHTOWER: Not me. I'm American.

VENTRIS TIDWELL: Well you look familiar.

SONNY HIGHTOWER: Damn right. *Long pause.* I can see, but I can't read.

VENTRIS TIDWELL: What you mean you can't read?

SONNY HIGHTOWER: I can't read. I told them that, and they said, We'll test him. See if that fucker can read or not. And they set me down in this room they got. And they started buzzing.

VENTRIS TIDWELL: Buzzing?

SONNY HIGHTOWER, *gaily:* Buzzing like fuckers. *The smile comes on again like a great light. His entire apperance changes. Before he seemed abstracted as though he was plugged in, listening to distant music on a Sony Walkman. Now he is focused the way a magnifying glass is focused. The smile feels like heat on his face, and Ventris Tidwell suddenly realizes he is angry. He feels the blood pound in his head. The language upsets him.*

VENTRIS TIDWELL: Goddamn it, I told you about that. *In a stage whisper:* Watch your language. This is a National Monument. It's like in church. You don't say things like that in church.

SONNY HIGHTOWER: Church. I stood that shit as long as I could, then I got up and walked around, and one of them fuckers said sit down, and I stepped out the window.

VENTRIS TIDWELL: You stepped out the window? *He can't beleive it.* What's your name? - *taking him by the arm.*

SONNY HIGHTOWER: U.S.

VENTRIS TIDWELL: U.S.? *He seems surprised.* U.S. what?

SONNY HIGHTOWER: U.S. Hightower. My Momma said, Call him Sonny.

VENTRIS TIDWELL: Sonny?

SONNY HIGHTOWER: Damn right. *Pauses.* I stepped out the window, and they yelled, Go get him, and one of them got me and said, Here read this, you say you can't read. And I said, I can't read. And they said, Read it. This is a test. So I buzzed at it, and they said, Out loud. Read it out loud. And I said, What the hell you call this, fucker? And they said, Read it where I can hear it and tell if you can read or not. So I buzzed at it louder, and they said. Hell, that ain't reading. And I said, Hell no. I told you that, fucker. And they said, He can't read. This guy's a moron, AndI said, Damm right. That's what I been trying to tell you. If I could read, I'd be in the army — *gesturing at the displays.*

VENTRIS TIDWELL: What you mean? You retarded or something?

SONNY HIGHTOWER: Damn right.

Long pause.

VENTRIS TIDWELL: Is that your real name?

SONNY HIGHTOWER: What?

VENTRIS TIDWELL: U.S. You named for Ulysses S. Grant or what? *It seems appropriate at Chick- kamauga, a moron named Ulysses S. Grant.*

SONNY HIGHTOWER: Looks like a red light. You

know how to drive?

VENTRIS TIDWELL: What?

Sonny Hightower points toward the display.

VENTRIS TIDWELL: I'll be damned. Look at that. Red and blue arrows. *Pauses.* Looks like some kind of traffic pattern, a cloverleaf on the Interstate. Red for stop. Green for go. *Then it comes to him.* Wait a minute. What you mean, green for go? The arrows are blue — *gesturing.*

SONNY HIGHTOWER: OK.

VENTRIS TIDWELL: OK what?

SONNY HIGHTOWER: OK, blue for go.

VENTRIS TIDWELL, *laughing*: Blue for go.

SONNY HIGHTOWER: Damn right. Blue for go. You got a sword?

VENTRIS TIDWELL: No.

SONNY HIGHTOWER: Me neither.

They fall silent again, contemplating the imaginary map.

VENTRIS TIDWELL: Interstates are weird damn places. One time I got caught in a fog and drove the Interstate all the way to Dalton before I knew where I was going. It was like a river. I was carried along by the current far past my destination. The cloverleaf shuttled the traffic, and the traffic moved on it wherever it went, going to its destination. Without the pattern it would all gridlock. Same thing with wars.

SONNY HIGHTOWER: Damn right. You ever kill

anybody?

Long pause.

VENTRIS TIDWELL: I don't know. *Abruptly:* What you mean, kill somebody?

SONNY HIGHTOWER: When you were in the army.

VENTRIS TIDWELL: How did you know I was in the army?

SONNY HIGHTOWER: The way you look. What's your name?

VENTRIS TIDWELL: Ventris.

SONNY HIGHTOWER: Ventris what?

VENTRIS TIDWELL: Ventris Tidwell.

SONNY HIGHTOWER: Ventris Tidwell — *as though testing it.* Don't sound like a name to me.

VENTRIS TIDWELL: My mother's maiden name — *lamely.*

SONNY HIGHTOWER: Sounds like it means something to me.

VENTRIS TIDWELL: That right?

SONNY HIGHTOWER: Sounds like it's somebody knocked on the door waiting to get in to me.

Ventris Tidwell nods his head.

SONNY HIGHTOWER: Sounds like U.S. to me.

VENTRIS TIDWELL, *quick as a rat in the wall:* U.S.? What you mean U.S.? *Pauses.* Well shit. Who was

Ulysses S. Grant?

SONNY HIGHTOWER: What you mean who was Ulysses S. Grant?

VENTRIS TIDWELL: I mean who was Ulysses S. Grant, you named for him like you say you are?

Long pause.

SONNY HIGHTOWER: Who gives a shit?

VENTRIS TIDWELL: That's what I figured.

SONNY HIGHTOWER: Ulysses S. Fucker Grant. Who gives a shit?

VENTRIS TIDWELL: Look here. *He goes over to the display case and taps on the glass.* U.S. Look at those canteens. U.S. This is a National Monument. Look here — *moving about the room.* It's all over the place. That ain't your name. You just made it up.

Sonny Hightower begins moving his hand in front of his face, slowly at first, then faster and faster, staring at the plan of battle.

VENTRIS TIDWELL: What's that? What are you doing? *Ventris Tidwell stares at the face moving through the blade of the hand. He seems fascinated, then begins shaking him.* Listen here — cut that out. I don't know if I killed anybody or not. I was in Nam.

SONNY HIGHTOWER: Nam what?

VENTRIS TIDWELL: Nam what? *He takes two vicious steps and returns.* Viet Nam. *He pronounces it to rhyme with jam.* You know. Viet Nam. Listen, you ever see that ad on TV? Poltician walking down the corridor of this prison. Bars on either side painted green. Whole place painted green. All of a sudden he stops in front of one of the cells and turns to the camera. "When I'm president," he says, grinning like he got a mouth full of shit, "I'm going to put all the criminals in jail." All of a sudden a guard runs up and slams the door. Makes a loud noise clanging and banging. Fucker's inside. They finally got the son of a bitch. That's what I think whenever I see it. They finally got the son of a bitch. He was not innocent.

Long pause. They stare at one another.

VENTRIS TIDWELL: Listen. The army took me, but I wish they hadn't. They liked to kill me.

SONNY HIGHTOWER: That's what they're supposed to do, ain't it?

VENTRIS TIDWELL: I don't mean *them.* I mean *me.* They liked to kill *me.*

SONNY HIGHTOWER: What's the difference?

VENTRIS TIDWELL: What's the difference? — *completely astonished.* There's all the difference in the world. Listen. They killed my brother.

SONNY HIGHTOWER: Who killed him?

VENTRIS TIDWELL: His own men. *He speaks as though in confidence, lowering his voice and leaning forward. Sonny Hightower leans back in the opposite direction.* The Americans. *Sonny Hightower is too far away to hear.*

SONNY HIGHTOWER: Who?

VENTRIS TIDWELL: His own men. Our own army. Americans. They thought he was somebody else.

SONNY HIGHTOWER: Who they think he was?

VENTRIS TIDWELL, *shouting, suddenly angry:*
How the hell do I know who they thought he was?
What does that matter?

SONNY HIGHTOWER: He's dead ain't he?

VENTRIS TIDWELL: What you mean? I just told
you he was dead, didn't I? His own fucking men killed
him.

SONNY HIGHTOWER: That's why it matters.

VENTRIS TIDWELL: Yes.

SONNY HIGHTOWER: If they knew who he was,
they might not have killed him. They know he was
your brother?

VENTRIS TIDWELL: What does that matter whose
fucking brother they thought he was? *He stops
suddenly.* They thought he was the Viet Cong.

SONNY HIGHTOWER: The Viet Cong? *He sounds
amazed as though he had just learned that Forest
Tidwell was believed to have been a Coca-Cola bottle.*
They thought he was the Viet Cong?

VENTRIS TIDWELL: You know what I mean?

SONNY HIGHTOWER: What?

VENTRIS TIDWELL: The Viet Cong. You know
what I mean?

Sonny Hightower looks about the room.

VENTRIS TIDWELL: Shit. They thought he was the
enemy.

*Sonny Hightower looks like someone put him in
neutral.*

VENTRIS TIDWELL: I mean the Americans. They thought he was the fucking enemy. His own men. You know what it was? *The words rise up like apparitions.* There wasn't even a body inside the coffin. They sealed it up and covered it with an American flag, and we didn't even know what was in it, it was so light.

SONNY HIGHTOWER: You mean there wasn't nothing there?

VENTRIS TIDWELL: They said, Don't open it. These are remains. His face was burned beyond recognition.

SONNY HIGHTOWER: You mean you didn't even get to see him? How'd you know who it was?

Ventris Tidwell does not reply.

SONNY HIGHTOWER: I said how'd you know who it was, you didn't even get to see him? It might have been the wrong one.

VENTRIS TIDWELL: Yes.

SONNY HIGHTOWER: What?

VENTRIS TIDWELL: It was the wrong one.

SONNY HIGHTOWER: They killed my brother with a car. They buried him, I knew who it was. I kissed his face, and they closed the lid, and I knew who was in there. That's how we're different.

VENTRIS TIDWELL: That's one way.

SONNY HIGHTOWER: What are the others?

VENTRIS TIDWELL: What others?

SONNY HIGHTOWER: The other ways we're

different.

VENTRIS TIDWELL: We ain't so different.

SONNY HIGHTOWER: Yours didn't die right. That's one way. You got an empty box. Mine was full. I know what I got.

Ventris Tidwell nods his head and starts to leave.

VENTRIS TIDWELL: That's one way. *He walks across the room and is almost out the door before Sonny Hightower realizes what is happening.*

SONNY HIGHTOWER, *shouting*: Wait a minute. Where are you going? *Running up to him*: What about reading? *He looks at him suspiciously.* Can you read?

VENTRIS TIDWELL: Yes.

SONNY HIGHTOWER: Read that. *He points above the heads of the audience at what we are to imagine as one of a series of large printed displays.*

VENTRIS TIDWELL, *reading*: "It was a haunted land...." How's that? What is this, some kind of test?

SONNY HIGHTOWER: Don't stop now! Keep on going. Read it out loud where I can hear it.

VENTRIS TIDWELL: "It was a haunted land. Chickamauga Creek was larger than most rivers in Europe. It flowed out of the mountains of North Georgia into the lowlands of Tennessee through a rough and broken country, a sparsely settled region of gloomy woods and lonely cabins. It had been given its name by the Indians — Chickamauga, the River of Death." You know what that means?

SONNY HIGHTOWER: Shit yeah.

VENTRIS TIDWELL: "For the early settlers who lived on its banks, it still retained that meaning, flowing in the heart of nature, eroding the edges of the fields and then suddenly rising up wild and uncontrollable sweeping away their loved ones and all their possessions."

As Ventris Tidwell reads, Sonny Hightower paces back and forth like an elephant chained to a stake. He mutters audibly to himself, echoing key words and phrases.

VENTRIS TIDWELL: "But the soldiers who arrived on its banks and began their blind, bitter struggle gave it a new meaning, baptizing it afresh with their blood. Marching, the armies sang the words of the old hymn, 'There is a Fountain Filled with Blood.' Chickamauga was that place."

SONNY HIGHTOWER: Don't stop! You ain't come to the end of it yet.

He walks up and peers at the display. He seems to be charmed by the words as snakes are said to be charmed by music.

SONNY HIGHTOWER: A fountain filled with blood.

VENTRIS TIDWELL: That's right.

SONNY HIGHTOWER: What else?

VENTRIS TIDWELL: That's it. That's all it says.

SONNY HIGHTOWER: Well shit. *He walks along the base of the wall as though looking for a way out. He comes to another display and stops.* What about that one? What's that one say?

VENTRIS TIDWELL, *reading:* "The Battle of

Chickamauga went to nobody's plan...."

Ventris Tidwell stops reading. Sonny Hightower comes up behind him as in the beginning. He stands there again like his shadow, then shouts at his back.

SONNY HIGHTOWER: Go on, read the fucker. Don't just stand there.

VENTRIS TIDWELL, *whirling about:* Don't ever do that again, I'll kill you.

SONNY HIGHTOWER: Go on, I'll kill you. *He gestures impatiently toward the display.*

VENTRIS TIDWELL: "The Battle of Chickamauga went to nobody's plan. A Brigadier General in the Union Army summed it up perfectly when he wrote that Chickamauga was 'a mad, irregular battle, very much resembling guerilla warfare on a vast scale in which one army was bushwacking the other and wherein all the science and art of war went for nothing. ' "

SONNY HIGHTOWER: Bushwacking. What's his name?

VENTRIS TIDWELL: Who?

SONNY HIGHTOWER: Guy said all that.

VENTRIS TIDWELL: I don't know.

SONNY HIGHTOWER: Well shit. Go on, read it.

VENTRIS TIDWELL: "The Battle of Chickamauga went to nobody's plan . . . ."

SONNY HIGHTOWER: Not there. Start where you left off.

VENTRIS TIDWELL: "The country was full of trees and underbrush with little clearings here and there; nobody could see much of his enemy's position, it was almost impossible to move artillery along the narrow country lanes, both armies were sodden with weariness, drinking water was hard to find, casualties were extremely heavy, and by nightfall all anyone could be sure of was that there had been a terrible fight and that it would be worse tomorrow."

Sonny Hightower begins pacing again, moving back and forth rhythmically, murmuring under his breath. It seems like a form of perseveration.

VENTRIS TIDWELL: "They were the two bloodiest days of American Military History. More than a quarter of the 124,000 men engaged were killed, wounded or missing; in some units casualties exceeded 80 percent."

— Bruce Catton

SONNY HIGHTOWER, *stopping suddenly as though arrested*: What?

VENTRIS TIDWELL: Bruce Catton.

SONNY HIGHTOWER: What's that mean?

VENTRIS TIDWELL: Man's name that wrote it. Some kind of general.

SONNY HIGHTOWER: That's what I figured. Why didn't you tell me?

VENTRIS TIDWELL: What? His name? How would I know? You think I read backwards?

SONNY HIGHTOWER: Well shit — *leaning forward to inspect the display more closely.* Don't ever do it again, you hear me?

*Sonny Hightower walks on down to the next display
and stands there inspecting it, looking out over the
audience as though praying or expecting to absorb the
message without reading it by simply remaining there
in its presence as some men practise the presence of
God. Ventris Tidwell joins him.*

SONNY HIGHTOWER, *leaning forward and
inspecting the grain of the display as one might inspect
the brush strokes of a painting*: What's it say?

VENTRIS TIDWELL, *reading*: "William S.
Rosencrans, Major General, U.S.A. Commanding, The
Army of Tennessee, Chattanooga Tennessee, to Henry
W. Halleck, Major General, U.S.A., General in Chief of
the Armies, War Office, Washington, D.C.
21 September 1863."

SONNY HIGHTOWER: Washington, D.C.

VENTRIS TIDWELL: "WE HAVE MET WITH A
SERIOUS DISASTER."

SONNY HIGHTOWER: "WE HAVE MET WITH A
SERIOUS DISASTER." *He seems delighted.*

VENTRIS TIDWELL: "EXTENT NOT YET
ASCERTAINED. ENEMY OVERWHELMED US.
DROVE OUR RIGHT, PIERCED OUR CENTER AND
SCATTERED TROOPS THERE. EVERY AVAILABLE
RESERVE WAS USED WHEN THE MEN
STAMPEDED. CHICKAMAUGA IS AS FATAL A
NAME IN OUR HISTORY AS BULL RUN."

SONNY HIGHTOWER: Bull Run. Goddamn. Look
how it looks. See that?

VENTRIS TIDWELL: Yes.

SONNY HIGHTOWER: Looks like a train whistle.

You know how to drive?

VENTRIS TIDWELL: Yes.

SONNY HIGHTOWER: Me too. I ain't forgot it. My brother taught me. They don't give you a license for driving unless you can read.

VENTRIS TIDWELL: I heard about that.

SONNY HIGHTOWER: I reckon so. Most folks have. *He waddles on down the wall like a rat moving along its base.*

VENTRIS TIDWELL: You know what that wall reminds me of? A wall they got in *The National Geographic* with all these pictures of men leaning their heads on it and sticking flowers in it or pieces of paper with messages on them. On the other side of the wall is nothing. It's not part of a building or something like that. It's just a wall.

Sonny Hightower keeps on going around the room and stops at the photographs at the rear of the stage.

SONNY HIGHTOWER: What about that one? What's that fucker looking like that for?

He points to a grainy photograph of a young man with a round face and slick hair that looks as though he had just combed it with water. He is wearing a bow tie and an open coat with large brass buttons running obliquely down his chest like bullet holes. His clothes look rumpled as though he had been sleeping in them. His face is plump and well-fed. In the crook of his left arm is a felt campaign hat with a large brass H on the front above the rim. The fingers holding the hat are tense.

VENTRIS TIDWELL, *coming up and reading the*

caption: "Sam R. Watkins, High Private, Company H, First Tennessee Regiment, Confederate States of America."

SONNY HIGHTOWER: What's it say?

VENTRIS TIDWELL: "I got of piece of cold corn dogger, laid my piece of the rat on it, eat a little piece of the bread, and raised the piece of rat to my mouth — Sam R. Watkins."

SONNY HIGHTOWER: Piece of rat. Well shit. *Pauses.* Looks like you don't it?

VENTRIS TIDWELL: Like me? Hell no. I don't look like that.

SONNY HIGHTOWER: Read what it says.

VENTRIS TIDWELL: "We remained on the battlefield of Chickamauga all night. Everything had fallen into our hands. We had captured a great many prisoners and small arms, and many pieces of artillery and wagons and provisions. Confederate and Federal dead, wounded, and dying, were everywhere scattered over the battlefield. Men were lying where they fell, shot in every conceivable part of the body. Some had their entrails torn and still hanging to them and piled up on the ground beside them, and they still alive."

SONNY HIGHTOWER: That's it. That's it. I know all about that. That's enough. *He waves his hand in front of his face like the blades of a chopper.*

VENTRIS TIDWELL: "Some with their underjaw torn off hanging by a fragment of skin to their cheeks, with their tongues lolling from their mouth."

Sonny Hightower touches his arm. Ventris Tidwell glances at him and continues to read.

VENTRIS TIDWELL: "Some with both eyes shot out, with one eye hanging down on their cheek. In fact, you might walk over the battlefield and find men shot from the crown of the head to the top of the toe. Dying on the field of battle and glory is about the easiest duty a soldier has to undergo. It is the living, fighting, shooting soldier that has the hardships to carry."

Sonny Hightower is holding his arm when he finishes. They look at one another a moment. Then Sonny Hightower detaches himself and wanders among the display cases.

SONNY HIGHTOWER: Look at this — *leaning on the display case.*

VENTRIS TIDWELL: What is it?

SONNY HIGHTOWER: I don't know.

VENTRIS TIDWELL: What's it look like?

SONNY HIGHTOWER: I don't know.

Ventris Tidwell goes over and looks.

VENTRIS TIDWELL: Canteens.

SONNY HIGHTOWER: Looks like looking in a mirror. See there.

Ventris Tidwell turns away with revulsion.

SONNY HIGHTOWER, *straightening up:* You got any more of them fuckers?

Ventris Tidwell looks about. He sees the photograph of the field of dead soldiers. He walks up to it and inspects it.

116

SONNY HIGHTOWER, *behind him again, looking over his shoulder*: What's that?

VENTRIS TIDWELL: Northern or Southern. You can't make them out. All jumbled up together. Papers, horses, pieces of wood, pots and pans, dead bodies.

SONNY HIGHTOWER: Dead bodies? What's it say?

VENTRIS TIDWELL, *reading the caption*: "Chickamauga."

SONNY HIGHTOWER: What's that mean?

VENTRIS TIDWELL: Chickamauga. The Battle of Chickamauga. This where it's at.

SONNY HIGHTOWER: That ain't here.

VENTRIS TIDWELL: Yes it is. That's where we are.

SONNY HIGHTOWER: Not me. That ain't where I am. Shit. *He laughs.* That all? You read them all?

VENTRIS TIDWELL: Except for the windows.

SONNY HIGHTOWER: The windows?

VENTRIS TIDWELL: A joke. I was making up a joke.

SONNY HIGHTOWER: A joke?

VENTRIS TIDWELL: Forget it.

SONNY HIGHTOWER: I mean that story. Any more about that story?

VENTRIS TIDWELL: What story?

SONNY HIGHTOWER: The one you were reading.

VENTRIS TIDWELL: Just the maps.

SONNY HIGHTOWER: Read that. *Pointing to an imaginary display:* What's that?

VENTRIS TIDWELL: A map.

SONNY HIGHTOWER: What's it say?

VENTRIS TIDWELL: 'Thomas's Corps.'

SONNY HIGHTOWER: What?

VENTRIS TIDWELL: 'Thomas's Corps.'

SONNY HIGHTOWER: What's that mean?

VENTRIS TIDWELL: It means where they went. The men in Thomas's command.

SONNY HIGHTOWER: Well shit. Read it.

VENTRIS TIDWELL: I already have. 'Thomas's Corps.' That's what it says.

Sonny Hightower goes closer and scrutinizes it, tracing the arrow.

SONNY HIGHTOWER: Thomas Corps. That's all it says?

VENTRIS TIDWELL: Listen. You don't read a map.

Sonny Hightower looks at him expectantly. He is like some sort of animal in a field — a mule or a horse or a cow.

VENTRIS TIDWELL: Maps show what happened . . . *He stops, knowing that is not it.* They're like diagrams. They show the movement.

SONNY HIGHTOWER: The movement.

VENTRIS TIDWELL: Yes. This is Thomas's Corps — *tracing an arrow.* And this is Longstreet's.

SONNY HIGHTOWER: Longstreets.

VENTRIS TIDWELL: Yes.

SONNY HIGHTOWER: Where's that?

VENTRIS TIDWELL: Here.

SONNY HIGHTOWER: That's Longstreets — *pointing.*

VENTRIS TIDWELL: That's right.

SONNY HIGHTOWER: What's Longstreets?

VENTRIS TIDWELL: Same as Thomas's — *suddenly angry.*

SONNY HIGHTOWER: Read it.

VENTRIS TIDWELL: I can't! *He starts to walk away, then comes back.* Listen. You don't know why you came here, and I don't know why I came here — *breaking off.* What time is it?

SONNY HIGHTOWER, *checking his watch:* Saturday.

VENTRIS TIDWELL: Saturday what?

Sonny Hightower looks confused.

VENTRIS TIDWELL: Saturday afternoon. What time is it? — *checking Sonny Hightower's watch.* Two forty-eight. How come you come here at two forty-eight on a Saturday afternoon and meet me?

SONNY HIGHTOWER: What?

VENTRIS TIDWELL: Same reason they did. They were marching around in the woods on and off the roads all day. Didn't know where they were going when all of a sudden they ended up here. And there was a reason. They died here or lived through the fighting to die somewhere else. And there was a reason. Like you and me. How come you come here? How come I come here? How come we met? That's what I mean. There's some kind of reason.

SONNY HIGHTOWER: What reason?

VENTRIS TIDWELL: What reason?

SONNY HIGHTOWER: Damn right. *Looking around*: What else you got?

VENTRIS TIDWELL: What else?

SONNY HIGHTOWER: Damn right. What else you got?

VENTRIS TIDWELL: That's all.

SONNY HIGHTOWER: That's what I figured. I'm much obliged. *Smiles.* Thank you for your kind assistance. *It sounds like a formula.*

VENTRIS TIDWELL: You're welcome.

Sonny Hightower continues to stand there. He seems about to say something. Then he walks across the room. He is just about to leave when he turns around and looks at Ventris Tidwell. He begins to wave goodbye the same way children wave goodbye, with his whole arm. Ventris Tidwell waves back. Sonny

Hightower suddenly drops his hand and starts back across the room.

VENTRIS TIDWELL, *seeing him come*: Oh shit. *Sonny Hightower is on him like a dog.*

SONNY HIGHTOWER: Now it's my turn to tell you a tale.

Sonny Hightower marches toward the center of the room. He holds his arms stiff at his side. When he reaches the middle, he stops and turns.

SONNY HIGHTOWER: Attention! — *coming stiffly to attention. The sound fills the room like an explosion.* Attention! This is the captain. We're going down. *He makes an elaborate sinking motion with his hand.* Who knows how to pray? *He pauses dramatically, then turns to Ventris Tidwell*: None of them know how to pray.

VENTRIS TIDWELL: Keep your voice down. Don't shout so loud. What if someone comes in here and wants to know what's happening? What am I going to tell them, you acting like that?

SONNY HIGHTOWER: No one could pray. *He has stepped out of the role he was playing. Then he stops and stands there, eyes shut, arms rigid at his side. He seems to have fallen into a trance. The tale or whatever it was — the recitation — is over.*

Long pause.

VENTRIS TIDWELL: That's some story. *He does not know what else to say. It seems like such a crazy, useless story. It's not even a joke. It's nothing.*

SONNY HIGHTOWER, *shouting suddenly*: All right. No one can pray. We'll take up an offering. *To Ventris*

Tidwell: You got a hat?

VENTRIS TIDWELL: What? *He has fallen down the rabbit hole.*

Sonny Hightower makes as though he is passing the hat.

SONNY HIGHTOWER, *shouting*: We took up the offering. Much obliged — *as though someone just gave him a hat full of money. He holds it in both hands and leans his face into it as into a mirror. Then he straightens up and shouts in a changed voice*: This is the captian. We're going down. *He steps out of the Role he was playing.* Then the ship sunk. They all died. *He gestures with his hand. It falls through the air like a leaf.* Now I told you a tale. *His eyes are still closed. He still stands at attention.*

VENTRIS TIDWELL: Much obliged. *He speaks automatically before he realizes he is angry.* Wait a minute. What's that mean? It wasn't money, that what you mean? *He stops abruptly.* What the hell you talking about, telling me something like that for?

Sonny Hightower remains standing rigidly at attention. His fists are clenched as though he is about to hit someone. His face is flushed. Ventris Tidwell watches as his mouth pulls back into his neck, baring his teeth. His whole body is like a muscle undergoing a massive contraction. A low sound rises from it as though forced out by the tremendous pressure. It is not the sound of a voice. It is the sound of the tissues themselves contracting. Ventris Tidwell becomes alarmed. He checks the door to see who is coming.

VENTRIS TIDWELL: Keep it down. *He rushes to Sonny Hightower and begins to shake him.* Shut up, Goddamn it. Somebody's coming. They're going to hear you. What are you doing?

Sonny Hightower falls over backwards and hits the display case. He slides off and scuttles about on the floo as though he is trying to creep under it. His arms and legs move in different directions. The heels of his shoes strike the floor in an irregular rhythm. His arms flail in angular motions, and his head starts to beat on the floor, lifting and falling. The moans increase. The volume is louder.

Ventris Tidwell begins to run. He is half-way across the room before he stops abruptly and comes back. He stands over Sonny Hightower, observing him.

VENTRIS TIDWELL, *angrily:* I could kill the son of a bitch. *He stoops suddenly and begins to frisk Sonny Hightower as though putting out a fire. The action is swift and violent. He rolls him over, locates his wallet, and tries to force it in his mouth. Sonny Hightower's teeth are clenched. His head flings itself about in his arms like an animal seeking release.*

VENTRIS TIDWELL: Son of a bitch. Hold still.

He crams the wallet in his mouth, then gets up and observes him again as though from a distance. Sonny Hightower continues the seizure. Ventris Tidwell turns and walks across the room. The irregular rhythm of the convulsion blends with the sound of his footsteps. When he comes to the door, he turns and looks across the room. Sonny Hightower is no longer moving. Ventris Tidwell reaches out and grasps the doorknob, holds it in his hand a moment, then turns and walks back across the room, the sound of his heels following him like a shadow.

Sonny Hightower's feet are sticking out from under the display case. Every so often they move as though he is trying to pull them inside after him. Ventris Tidwell drops to his knees and peers under the case.

SONNY HIGHTOWER: What are you doing?

VENTRIS TIDWELL: I don't know. *Pauses.* I don't know what I'm doing.

SONNY HIGHTOWER: I do.

VENTRIS TIDWELL: What?

SONNY HIGHTOWER: Looking at me.

VENTRIS TIDWELL: That's right — *laughing.* I came back to see how you are.

SONNY HIGHTOWER: Back from where?

VENTRIS TIDWELL: I don't know. Nowhere. How are you feeling?

SONNY HIGHTOWER: Fine as wine. How are you?

VENTRIS TIDWELL: Fine as wine.

SONNY HIGHTOWER: What happened?

VENTRIS TIDWELL: I don't know. An accident.

SONNY HIGHTOWER: Where am I?

VENTRIS TIDWELL: Under the table. You want to get out?

SONNY HIGHTOWER: Sure.

VENTRIS TIDWELL: Give me your leg. *He starts to pull him out by the leg, but Sonny Hightower kicks him away. He tries to stand up by himself only to discover that the top of the case will not allow it.*

SONNY HIGHTOWER: I can't stand up — *shouting.*

It's all over me. I can't move!

Ventris Tidwell drops to his knees and crawls under the display case. He wrestles Sonny Hightower to the floor.

VENTRIS TIDWELL, *breathing heavily*: Kneel down. Follow me. Look here, like this. *He crawls out. Sonny Hightower emerges a few moments later. He continues to crawl until Ventris Tidwell puts a hand on his shoulder and stops him.* Can you stand up?

SONNY HIGHTOWER: I don't know you.

VENTRIS TIDWELL: You want to try? You want me to help you?

SONNY HIGHTOWER: Sure.

Ventris Tidwell bends over and tries to heave him upright. Sonny Hightower twists around in his arms, trying to get a glimpse of his face.

SONNY HIGHTOWER: Who are you?

VENTRIS TIDWELL: Who am I? *He does not quite know what to say.* A friend.

SONNY HIGHTOWER: A friend. Where am I?

VENTRIS TIDWELL: Chickamauga.

SONNY HIGHTOWER: What?

VENTRIS TIDWELL: Chickamauga. Where they had the battle of Chickamauga.

SONNY HIGHTOWER: Chickamauga. I already been.

VENTRIS TIDWELL: You look like you been — *laughing.*

SONNY HIGHTOWER: Fucker already read it to me. You ready to go? Let's go.

VENTRIS TIDWELL: Go? Go where?

SONNY HIGHTOWER: Outside. This full of shit.

VENTRIS TIDWELL: What? You all right?

SONNY HIGHTOWER: Shit yeah.

VENTRIS TIDWELL: I mean your pants. You soil yourself?

SONNY HIGHTOWER: Shit yeah.

VENTRIS TIDWELL: What? You do something in there?

SONNY HIGHTOWER: Where?

VENTRIS TIDWELL: In there — *gesturing.*

SONNY HIGHTOWER: Hell no. Let's go. It's time to go.

VENTRIS TIDWELL: That's right — *laughing.* It's time to go.

He stands up and offers to help Sonny Hightower. Sonny Hightower waves him off and struggles upright himself. He stands there swaying.

SONNY HIGHTOWER: What you mean, soil yourself?

Ventris Tidwell reaches out and steadies him.

VENTRIS TIDWELL: You all right?

SONNY HIGHTOWER: Damn right. You take my arm. You going to help me, that's how you do it. You carry my arm.

Ventris Tidwell carries his arm.

SONNY HIGHTOWER: My pins ain't steady.

VENTRIS TIDWELL: Your pins?

SONNY HIGHTOWER: The pins on my feet. They're coming loose. My feet feel like they're wobbling off.

VENTRIS TIDWELL: You want to sit down?

SONNY HIGHTOWER: Hell no. I got a tale I'll tell you about that.

VENTRIS TIDWELL: About what?

SONNY HIGHTOWER: The pins on my feet. You want to hear it?

VENTRIS TIDWELL: Not yet.

SONNY HIGHTOWER, *agreeing*: Not yet. It's too early.

VENTRIS TIDWELL: Shit yeah — *smiling*. How you feeling?

SONNY HIGHTOWER: Gooder than snuff. How're you?

VENTRIS TIDWELL, *smiling*: Gooder than snuff. You want to open the door?

SONNY HIGHTOWER: Shit yeah. *He moves forward and tries to push it open with his hands, then with his shoulder. The door will not move. He turns and looks at Ventris Tidwell.*

VENTRIS TIDWELL: Pull. *He moves forward to help him. They pull together. The door opens, and the sunlight is momentarily blinding.* Look at the sky. It's so bright, I can't even see it. *To Sonny Hightower:* Come on.

SONNY HIGHTOWER: Where we going?

VENTRIS TIDWELL: That clump of oaks over there. Then on down the hill to the row of trees along the river.

SONNY HIGHTOWER: What river?

VENTRIS TIDWELL: The Chickamauga. See there? See where it's shining?

SONNY HIGHTOWER: Where?

VENTRIS TIDWELL: Over there. See that flash?

SONNY HIGHTOWER: I see it. What is it?

VENTRIS TIDWELL: We don't know yet. Some kind of glory.

They walk through the door. The stage is left empty.

Martial music as in the beginning.

The light gradually fades into darkness.

PART THREE

The Call Of Nature

SCENE

Two P.M. Saturday Afternoon. The Gateway Shopping Center.

CAST OF CHARACTERS

DORTIS MULKEY, a car thief
LUCILLE ARP, an old woman

The stage is empty except for the stylized frame of an automobile. Dortis Mulkey enters and checks it out. It is obvious he intends to steal it. He sees no one looking, grabs the keys, jumps in and drives off. Sound of tires screeching.

LUCILLE ARP, *rising up like an apparition from behind the front seat:* Where we going?

It is like the voice of God. Dortis Mulkey loses control. The car leaps out of his hands. He struggles for control.

LUCILLE ARP: I said where we going? You from the car wash?

DORTIS MULKEY: Yes Ma'am — *obviously lying.*

LUCILLE ARP: What?

Dortis Mulkey checks it out in the rear view mirror. A figure of some sort against the light. Face black in shadows. Hair smokey, electrified. Old voice.

DORTIS MULKEY: Yes Ma'am.

LUCILLE ARP: What? Young man like you. Deaf

already. You can't hear a thing I'm saying. I have to shout, and that makes me tired.

DORTIS MULKEY, *shouting:* Yes Ma'am.

LUCILLE ARP: That's better. I can hear you better now. You hear what I say?

DORTIS MULKEY: Yes Ma'am.

LUCILLE ARP: Well then why don't you?

DORTIS MULKEY: Do what?

LUCILLE ARP: Quit the car wash — *leaning forward, breath hot on Dortis Mulkey's neck.* I been looking for a young man like you.

Dortis Mulkey turns to look at her. The right wheel drops off the pavement onto the shoulder of the road and shudders before he rights it again. She is older than he thought.

LUCILLE ARP: I been wanting to go home. I been looking for a young man to drive me.

DORTIS MULKEY: This your car?

LUCILLE ARP: It's Hollis' car.

DORTIS MULKEY: Who's Hollis?

LUCILLE ARP: Charlene's husband — *as though he was a fool to have asked.* They gone shopping. You know how to get to Unadilla?

DORTIS MULKEY: No, Ma'am.

LUCILLE ARP: Roll up the window and turn on the air. It's blowey back here. You're driving too fast. Now listen. The way we get there is go to Macon. You on the Macon road?

DORTIS MULKEY: Not yet.

LUCILLE ARP: Well get on the Macon Road. Go on through till you come to Perry. You know where that's at? Of course you do. Drivers know the Macon road. Homer could find it if he was here. You set Homer down in the deserts of Outer Mongolia and give him a car, he'd find that road. That's why I love him. You know where it is, don't you? Of course you do. Young man like you. Been driving for two or three years, I reckon.

DORTIS MULKEY: Two years — *obviously insulted.* I been driving since I was eight. There ain't nothing I can't drive. They ain't made it. Or fix it neither one. I can drive a bulldozer and backhoe both. I can drive a eighteen wheeler if I had me one. Driving's my hobby. I purely love it.

LUCILLE ARP: Me, too. Homer too. He loved it too.

DORTIS MULKEY: There ain't nothing I like better than getting in a car and going.

LUCILLE ARP: That's right. We used to go every Sunday after dinner, down this road and that. I been down every road in Houston and Pulaski counties twenty-five times. You turn here? There's a paved road to the left. That one goes to Macon, don't it?

DORTIS MULKEY: Talking Rock. That one goes to Talking Rock.

LUCILLE ARP: Well, you know where it's at. Smart young man like you. Drive anything. I can't even drive. Old as I am, I never did know how. Homer got sick, and I couldn't drive him. I blame myself. I had him in my arms in the front seat. I got him that far. I tried to get him to show me how to get to the hospital. Heart. It was his heart, else he might still be here with me now, living in Unadilla in my own house instead of with Charlene. It takes a man for some things, I reckon, and driving is one. That's why I am so glad I got you — *leaning forward to pat Dortis Mulkey's shoulder.* Rooster? That you Rooster? — *as though seeing him for the first time. He is turned around in the seat facing her.* I didn't know you were Rooster.

DORTIS MULKEY: I ain't.

LUCILLE ARP, *ignoring him:* Thank God you came. You're going to drive me to Unadilla.

DORTIS MULKEY: Unadilla?

LUCILLE ARP: What? — *shouting.* Speak up. Don't mumble like the rest of them. You're still a young man. Speak out crisply. That's what I used to tell my students. Speak out crisply, and stand up beside your desk when you talk. What you say your name was anyway?

DORTIS MULKEY, *shouting:* Tarbaby.

LUCILLE ARP: Tarbaby! What kind of name is that? That ain't your real name. What your folks call you?

DORTIS MULKEY: Rickey. Rickey Mulkey.

LUCILLE ARP: Rickey Mulkey — *rolling the words around in her mouth.* That's all right. I like that. I like that name. It ends on a high note.

DORTIS MULKEY: What's that supposed to mean? What you mean high note?

LUCILLE ARP: Way it sounds. I like it. Sounds like

a scream.

DORTIS MULKEY: Scream?

LUCILLE ARP: Like somebody shouting pinned in the wreckage.

DORTIS MULKEY: Wreckage?

LUCILLE ARP: If they were in an accident from driving too fast.

Dortis Mulkey looks at the speedometer and immediately takes his foot off the accelerator and touches the brake, scanning the rear view mirror for police.

LUCILLE ARP: Rickey's all right. What's your momma call you?

DORTIS MULKEY: Rickey. That's my name ain't it?

LUCILLE ARP: No it ain't. You got some kind of family name.

DORTIS MULKEY: Dortis. Dortis Mulkey. *It is as though he had been touched in the heart with an icicle. His mouth opens and the name appears.* That's my real name. Rickey's what I call myself. Every year I go to school, they ask me my name and I say Rickey, and they all say, Bubba. That ain't Rickey. That's Bubba Mulkey. And the teacher says, Hush up. That's baby talk, Bubba and Sister, and such as that. We don't use them. And she calls me Dortis. Had it written down on a card. Dortis Mulkey. Just like my momma. How you know that?

LUCILLE ARP: No momma in her right mind would name a child of hers Rickey. That's one thing. Rickey's some kind of fool name. It ain't got no weight. Besides which, it's my gift.

DORTIS MULKEY: What gift is that — *checking the speed again.*

LUCILLE ARP: My gift — *disinterested.* This the road to Macon? We onto it yet?

DORTIS MULKEY: Yes Ma'am — *obviously lying.*

LUCILLE ARP: That's all right then. *Long pause. When she speaks again, she speaks more briskly as though having come to a resolution.* I got a special gift of God. I was born with it. I was born with a prophet's mantle. You know what that is?

DORTIS MULKEY: No Ma'am.

LUCILLE ARP: You're born with it — like gauze on your face covering your eyes. My momma told me, "Lucille, you got the special gift of sight called a prophet's mantle. Comes from God."

DORTIS MULKEY: What's it do?

LUCILLE ARP: It sees the future. It knows what it is before it happens. I saw you coming.

DORTIS MULKEY, *crying in anguish*: Me? That's what I figured.

LUCILLE ARP, *interrupting*: I knew he wouldn't let me stay on with Hollis. I figure God loves me too much for that. I knew he was fixing to send a servant to drive me home, seeing as I can't do it myself. You know why that was?

DORTIS MULKEY: I don't know and I don't want to.

LUCILLE ARP: To free us both. You from stealing cars and me from Hollis. And look at us now, driving like birds on the road to Macon, going South where the warm weather is. Going home.

Long pause during which Lucille Arp begins singing. The words drift weightlessly inside the car. "Love lifted me," she sings. It is the old hymn.

LUCILLE ARP:
> Love lifted me! Love lifted me!
> When nothing else could help, Love lifted me.
>
> I was sinking deep in sin
> Far from the peaceful shore,
> Very deeply stained within
> Sinking to rise no more;
>
> But the Master of the sea
> Heard my despairing cry
> From the waters lifted me
> Now safe am I.
>
> Love lifted me! Love lifted me!
> When nothing else could help, Love lifted me.

LUCILLE ARP: You ever been to Unadilla?

DORTIS MULKEY: No, Ma'am — *as though in pain.* O God, you ever feel like you had to do something no matter if you wanted to or not — like that song you were just singing? Say I'm driving a eighteen wheeler, except it ain't me. It's somebody else doing the driving. And I'm the gears. First, second, third, fourth — right on through the sequence. Whatever they are I got to go through them because I ain't driving, you know what I mean? It's somebody else doing the driving. Hold on — *loudly.*

LUCILLE ARP: What for?

DORTIS MULKEY: We're turning here. We got turned around back there. This is the road to Snellville. It don't go to Unadilla.

LUCILLE ARP: That's what I thought. I thought you were going the wrong way. Get on the road to Macon first. That's the one going to get you there. You hear what I say?

DORTIS MULKEY: Yes, Ma'am. We're going now.

LUCILLE ARP: That's good. You're going to love it. I got me a house there painted white and a place for a garden and shade trees Homer planted when we were first married and a glider and spring chairs under them he painted white every year. That's where you can sit and rest when you get done driving. You stay with me. Help me get set up. You hear me, Rooster? You can sleep in your own room. You hear that, honey? I kept it for you just like it was. *She pats his shoulder.*

Dortis Mulkey swerves at the touch. Then the car falls into line.

DORTIS MULKEY: Rooster? Who's Rooster?

Lucille Arp does not answer.

DORTIS MULKEY: Set up? Set up in what? Sounds to me like you're set up already.

LUCILLE ARP: I am for living, but not for business. I mean for business. Set up in that.

DORTIS MULKEY: What business?

LUCILLE ARP: Reader Adviser. You can paint the sign and take care of the advertising. That's one reason we got the car, that and the fact it's the way to get there. This car's going to come in handy. You can go from house to house drumming up business, putting notes in mail boxes and knocking on doors, telling them come. All they got to do is come and it shall be known. Pull over here — *pointing.*

DORTIS MULKEY: What for?

LUCILLE ARP: The call of nature.

Noise of car pulling off the road.

LUCILLE ARP: Not here.

Dortis Mulkey whirls about in the seat facing her.

LUCILLE ARP: I ain't no man to go in the bushes. I mean down there in the filling station.

Car starts up again.

LUCILLE ARP: There it is. *She struggles to free herself of the car.* Wait here — *flapping her elbow like a wing for assistance.*

Dortis Mulkey graps her arm and draws her out into the daylight. She is frail and knotty as a handful of kindling.

LUCILLE ARP: Wait here. I won't be a minute — *starts to leave, comes back almost immediately and removes the keys, then exits. Dortis Mulkey fidgets and waits, gets out of the car, walks around it, and gets back in. He sits there for a while, then begins to sing softly to himself.*

DORTIS MULKEY:
    Love lifted me! Love lifted me.
    When nothing else could help, Love lifted me.

LUCILLE ARP, *appearing suddenly at the window:* There ain't no towels. My face is all wet. Help me in. I feel a whole lot better now. There ain't but one thing better than washing your face.

DORTIS MULKEY: What's that?

LUCILLE ARP: Breathing. Let's get going. I got a heap of things to do.

She flings herself at the back seat, struggling to get in.

DORTIS MULKEY: You're going to hurt yourself — *leaping out to help her.*

LUCILLE ARP: You're too slow — *handing him the keys.* We're wasting time. Get on to Macon, and I'll show you from there. *She starts to sing again.*

> Some glad morning when this life is o'er,
> I'll fly away;
> To a home on God's celestial shore,
> I'll fly away.

Dortis Mulkey joins in the chorus tentatively at first, then more fully, with gusto.

> I'll fly away,
> O glory,
> I'll fly away;
> When I die, hallelujah, by and by,
> I'll fly away.

Lucille Arp sings the last verse alone. Dortis Mulkey joins in the refrain and the chorus:

> When the shadows of this life have gone,
> I'll fly away;
> Like a bird from prison bars has flown,

I'll fly away.

Chorus.

> Just a few more weary days and then,
> I'll fly away;
> To a land where joy shall never end,
> I'll fly away.

Chorus.

DORTIS MULKEY: What's your name?

LUCILLE ARP: Princess Mosak.

DORTIS MULKEY: Princess Mosak! That ain't your real name.

LUCILLE ARP: Of course it ain't. I was born Lucille Arp. Princess Mosak's the name I got now. Princess Mosak, Reader Adviser.

DORTIS MULKEY: What's that mean? Reader Adviser.

LUCILLE ARP: Reader means I read the signs.

DORTIS MULKEY: The signs?

LUCILLE ARP: Adviser means I give advice. I was sitting in the glider one afternoon watching the yellow jackets eat a piece of watermelon Homer left when he went for the salt. I was feeling the heat when it came to me. Princess Mosak. Just like that. Princess Mosak. As soon as I heard it, I knew it was me, like I am inside. Because of my gift. Princess Mosak, that's the name of it — the name of the gift.

She leans forward and touches Dortis Mulkey on the shoulder. His head shoots sideways as though struck

*by an electric current. He is trying to see her face in
the darkness.*

LUCILLE ARP: It was God. He gave me the gift, and
then he gave me the name for it, the way I feel inside.
Princess Mosak.

DORTIS MULKEY: O God — *car screeches as he
loses control.*

LUCILLE ARP, *ignoring him:* I ain't paid it enough
attention. I was too busy. Things come to me, I'd be
washing the dishes, you think I'd put them down and
dry my hands and go over there and tell them about
it? It's like good deeds. Like loving gestures. You think
of them. You feel it stirring to give them some plea-
sur, show them how much you love them maybe, and
then you don't do it. I don't know why. Time passes. It
slips away. I'd finish the dishes and dry my hands and go
out and sit with Homer and rock in the spring chair or
swing in the glider, and then I'd forget it. I'd let it slide. I
never even told Homer or Rooster. Not even what I saw
at the end.

DORTIS MULKEY: Who's Rooster?

LUCILLE ARP: My only child. My loving baby. I
never even told him.

DORTIS MULKEY: What about Hollis owns this car?

LUCILLE ARP: He ain't mine. He'd burn the house
down and me in it if he had his own way. I told
Charlene, and she said, "You mean to tell me my
husband's an arsonist? And all I said was, "You said it
not me." That which cometh to pass, if it ain't now, it
will be, and if it has been, it may be in time to come.
Charlene don't know about that.

DORTIS MULKEY: How come Rooster's your only

child if you got a daughter named Charlene married to
Hollis?

LUCILLE ARP: She came later. Rooster died. Had a
wolf in him, ate him inside and killed him and ate me
too and killed me for two years till I had Charlene,
and I never even told him. I just held on to his hand
and wept where he couldn't hear me, and then he was
dead, and I could have told him. He died in peace, but
I could have told him. I could have cried, "Watch out,"
and not let him die. All my life I had the gift and
never did use it for good or evil. I let it rot like a rag in
the water, sloshing this way and that, wearing itself
out with the motion. And I could have helped them.
Think of all the good I could have done. I had the gift
the Lord gave me like a bright flame, and I took it and
put it under a bushel. I buried it out in the side yard
under the trees sitting with Homer instead of getting
up and going about the Lord's business.

DORTIS MULKEY: The Lord's business! What's
that?

LUCILLE ARP: Making them happy. Giving them
warnings and advice. That's what I'm here for. The
Lord sent me like a prophet of old — like messenger
angels.

DORTIS MULKEY: What about me? You got some
kind of message for me? You know what I'm fixing to
do?

LUCILLE ARP: We're coming to that. Drive the car.
*Long pause. She hums to herself and looks out the
window at the dark landscape fleeting past.* I knew
you were coming — *as though speaking to herself.*
Ever since Homer died, I knew you were coming.
"Come home, Princess Mosak," it said. "Come home."
And I knew you were coming.

DORTIS MULKEY: It knew I was coming!

LUCILLE ARP: Of course it did. You or somebody
else just like you. Whoever the good Lord saw fit to
send and give him the talent.

DORTIS MULKEY: What talent?

LUCILLE ARP: The talent of driving and knowing
the way and helping me set it up when we get there.
Driving the car and advertising.

DORTIS MULKEY: Princess Mosak — *as though the
judge had just pronounced sentence.*

LUCILLE ARP: That's right. If it hadn't been you,
it'd been someone else, and if it hadn't been someone
else, it'd been you. And it was. You were chosen. Of all
the people in the world, the good Lord picked you in
his infinite wisdom.

DORTIS MULKEY: Why me? O God, why me?

LUCILLE ARP: You're the agent — *losing interest.*
We ain't talking about that anyway. We're talking
about me and what I'm fixing to do when I get there. I
been redeemed. I been freed of the bondage of Egypt.
I'm passing over. Pharoah's chariots drown in the
water, and I keep on going. There ain't no stopping me
now. I'm going home. My whole life has been
redeemed. I get to start over. I get to do it right this
time. *Sings again:* "Just a few more weary days and
then, / I'll fly away."

DORTIS MULKEY, *interrupting*: What about me? *It
sounds like a cry of pain.*

LUCILLE ARP: You're free ain't you? Why you
think you're riding with me, if you ain't been set free?
If it wasn't for having to drive me home, you might

146

have to spend the rest of your life stealing cars. But look at you now. You don't even know where you're going. That's how free you are.

DORTIS MULKEY: Here, tell my fortune — *thrusting a hand over the back of the seat. What you see there? — holding the hand palm up as though asking for alms.*

LUCILLE ARP: That ain't how to do it — *moving the hand aside.*

DORTIS MULKEY: What is it? What you see I'm fixing to do?

LUCILLE ARP: I wait for a sign. Something tells me.

DORTIS MULKEY: Tells what? — *searching her face in the darkness.*

LUCILLE ARP: This and that. Whatever comes to me. I ever tell you about the Unadilla girls' basketball team?

Dortis Mulkey's mind is somewhere else.

LUCILLE ARP: Won the State Championship. Fifteen or twenty years ago. I had those girls in my class. All in the same class, looking this way and that like some kind of puzzle got lines going every which a way. Call on them, they'd look at the blackboard. And I saw them looking, I got right up and went down the hall and told the coach, Mary Dewey. Skinny girl. Calves of her legs bunched like a man's. Ever see that?

Dortis Mulkey does not reply. He is staring straight ahead as though he saw something afar, at the farthest limit and point of the road. Lucille Arp punches him in the middle of the back.

LUCILLE ARP: Ever see a woman's leg bunched like a man's fist?

Dortis Mulkey leaps from the seat. Car screeches out of control.

LUCILLE ARP: That's how Mary Dewey's were. I figure it must have been all that coaching made them like that. Mine are smooth. Always have been. Round as an egg. Hers looked like a bunch of grapes. Mary Dewey. Dead now. *Pauses.* They're all dead. Gone into the sky like stars. I see the stars, I think of them shining. Sometimes I think that.

DORTIS MULKEY: I never have.

LUCILLE ARP: You're too young, that's why. All your loved ones ain't dead already except Charlene and the children, and they're all gone over to Hollis. All except you. *She pats him on the shoulder.* You're still with me, ain't you honey?

DORTIS MULKEY: What about the State Championship?

LUCILLE ARP: I'm coming to that. Don't rush me. I told Mary Dewey, "You got you a State Championship sitting right there in the study hall last period if you only knew it." And she said, "How's that — snippy-like, the way she talked — fast and snippy. And I said, "I saw them looking." And I told her what it was, and she got them and trained them, and they won the State Championship two years in a row. Nobody knew where they were looking. Look here and shoot there. All five of them. Every cross-eyed girl in town. Natural born basketball players. Couldn't figure them out, which way they were going.

DORTIS MULKEY: That's good — *losing interest.*

LUCILLE ARP: That's how signs are. Look one way and go the other. Took me to tell them or else they'd still be a bunch of ugly girls instead of a State Championship basketball team bringing back glory, and you know what else?

DORTIS MULKEY: No Ma'am — *not listening.*

LUCILLE ARP: Every one of them girls got married within the year. How about that? That's five I made happy. If it wasn't for me, nobody'd even think about marrying them. Sit on the porch waving at cars the rest of their life if it wasn't for me. Ugly girls got a hard life.

DORTIS MULKEY: Damn right — *suddenly coming alive.* Ugly boys too.

LUCILLE ARP: What are you talking about? You ain't ugly.

DORTIS MULKEY: Yes I am. I got bumps all over my neck.

LUCILLE ARP: That ain't nothing. I used to be ugly, but Homer married me anyway because he had good sense. All my life I had blessing on blessing as long as he lived. Some day you're going to get married too — *leaning forward to pat Dortis Mulkey on the shoulder.*

DORTIS MULKEY: No Ma'am. I love girls. I purely love them. But I don't aim to marry one.

LUCILLE ARP: What you aim to do with them then?

DORTIS MULKEY: I aim to race. Girls don't like that.

LUCILLE ARP: Why not? Ain't nothing wrong with

athletics even after you get out of school. Most girls don't mind.

DORTIS MULKEY: I mean cars. You think I meant running a race on my feet? I don't run.

LUCILLE ARP: You mean automobiles like this one?

DORTIS MULKEY: No Ma'am. I mean stock cars. Track racing. Special built.

LUCILLE ARP: How fast you going? Check your speed.

Dortis Mulkey obeys without thinking.

DORTIS MULKEY: That's what I mean. Women think you're going to get killed. That's why I don't plan to get married till after I retire. Women hold you back. You ain't free, you got a woman holding you back. Track racing's safer than highway driving.

LUCILLE ARP: I don't doubt it. It ain't safe nowhere. *Sings to herself:*

> I am living now in Canaan,
> Where the fruit so richly grows,
> Where the saints are all rejoicing,
> Where the milk and honey flows.

Dortis Mulkey begins to join in with the chorus of "I'll Fly Away." Lucille Arp joins him.

LUCILLE ARP: You hungry?

DORTIS MULKEY: Yes Ma'am. They say I stay hungry.

LUCILLE ARP: Who says that?

150

DORTIS MULKEY: Everybody. I say it myself.

LUCILLE ARP: You eat everything?

DORTIS MULKEY: Everything that's food.

LUCILLE ARP: I mean food. You think I meant seat upholstery?

DORTIS MULKEY: No, Ma'am.

LUCILLE ARP: What you like best to eat?

DORTIS MULKEY: Hard boiled eggs and corn bread.

LUCILLE ARP: You're kind of unusual in that. You like them together?

DORTIS MULKEY: Yes, Ma'am. I eat them for breakfast. That's my favorite breakfast food.

LUCILLE ARP: I like oatmeal. That's all I eat, oatmeal and sugar cookies. Charlene worries, says, "Momma, eat something else or you're going to get hookworm." And I say, "Don't worry. Hookworm don't come in at the mouth." I figure I got a right to eat what I want to, old as I am.

DORTIS MULKEY: Where you want to go? We're going anywhere you want to go.

LUCILLE ARP, *suspiciously:* You mean somewhere like eating oatmeal?

DORTIS MULKEY: No Ma'am. I mean the whole world — *lifting his right hand from the steering wheel and gesturing beyond the windshield at the scattered landscape.*

LUCILLE ARP: The whole world. You mean the whole world?

DORTIS MULKEY: Yes, Ma'am. Where you want to go?

LUCILLE ARP: I don't know. . . . Wait a minute. Give me a minute. I can't think. . . . Indian Springs! We used to go to Indian Springs. Homer and I used to go there.

DORTIS MULKEY: What was it like?

LUCILLE ARP: Sat on the porch — *remembering.* In the evening. They had these rockers on the veranda. Green floor. Forest green. And you take the waters.

DORTIS MULKEY: Where you take them?

LUCILLE ARP: You drink them, you ignorant boy. What grade you in?

DORTIS MULKEY: No grade. I quit — *trying not to feel the end of the rope.* I used to drink water all the time except I wouldn't go there to do it.

LUCILLE ARP: These special waters. Taste like sulphur.

DORTIS MULKEY: What tastes like sulphur? You mean the water? *The information galvanizes him.*

LUCILLE ARP: Some taste like iron. And tomatoes. The iron one tasted like tomatoes to me.

DORTIS MULKEY: They got one taste like squash? Fried squash and onions? They got one tastes like fried squash and onions?

LUCILLE ARP: Across the road was the Indian house — *remembering.* Chief McIntosh. He was a half-breed. Had a stuffed horse in the bedroom.

DORTIS MULKEY: Had a what?

LUCILLE ARP: Had a stuffed horse in the bedroom.

DORTIS MULKEY: What for?

LUCILLE ARP: It died, and they stuffed it. I don't have to tell you why. I ain't accountable for that.

DORTIS MULKEY: You want to go there? Let's go right now. That's one thing I'd love to see, a horse in a bedroom. I'd rather see that than Paris, France.

LUCILLE ARP: It ain't there. Burned down. Hotel burned, and the museum rotted.

DORTIS MULKEY: Then in that case there ain't no sense going. Let's go to Six Flags Over Georgia.

LUCILLE ARP: I been already. *Pauses.* I been everywhere there is to go.

DORTIS MULKEY: Where's that? Give me a for instance.

Lucille Arp pauses, thinking.

LUCILLE ARP: Shoulderbone Mounds — *suddenly.* I been to Shoulderbone Mounds, near Sparta.

DORTIS MULKEY: Mounds? What you mean mounds?

LUCILLE ARP: You ignorant boy. I wish I had you in my class. You ain't never heard of Shoulderbone Mounds and Irene? Okmulgee, and Etowah Mounds?

All them famous mounds in the state?

DORTIS MULKEY: No Ma'am. I though you were talking about Mounds candy bars.

LUCILLE ARP: I did a whole section on mounds. Every spring. Ain't a person in Unadilla didn't know about Shoulderbone Mounds. The ones I didn't teach learned from the others, parent from child and darkey from white. They know all about it.

DORTIS MULKEY: Yes, Ma'am. I must have missed that.

LUCILLE ARP: Not all teaches it.

DORTIS MULKEY: What's it look like? It look hairy or what?

LUCILLE ARP, *remembering*: We got there, it was a grist mill. The man that owned it worked at the grist mill on the Little Shoulderbone Creek, and he took us — Homer and me. Got in his pickup, me in the front and Homer in a chair in the bed, and drove through the woods and the fields where they used to grow cotton, all in weeds and cockleburrs, and then we came to it.

DORTIS MULKEY: What was it — *unable to contain himself.*

LUCILLE ARP: The mounds. Out in the fields, rising up out of the weeds. And we had the map from Colonel Jones and found the spring they used, and the burial mound and the platform mound, where they had the temple, and the plaza where they danced, and the moat. It was all there under the weeds.

DORTIS MULKEY: Yes Ma'am — *suddenly disinterested.* Where else you been?

LUCILLE ARP: That man that owned it had a button — *still remembering.*

DORTIS MULKEY: That right?

LUCILLE ARP: Said it was made out of an Indian's ear.

DORTIS MULKEY: A what? *It is as though someone grasped him by the hair and pulled him out of the water.*

LUCILLE ARP: A button made out of an Indian's ear. Said his granddaddy wore it on his vest.

DORTIS MULKEY: What for?

LUCILLE ARP: To hear when they're coming. The Indian Nation began on the other side of the river, and he wore the ear to know when they're coming.

DORTIS MULKEY: Where did he get it?

LUCILLE ARP: I didn't ask him. Off a dead Indian, I reckon. He must have found one dead and cut off his ear.

DORTIS MULKEY: If he didn't kill him — *suddenly aflame again.* Where is it? They still got it? I'd give a whole lot to see a button made out of an Indian's ear. What's it look like?

LUCILLE ARP: Not much. Like pigskin. White like pigskin after the hair's off. I wouldn't have known what it was if he hadn't told me.

DORTIS MULKEY: You mean it didn't look like an ear?

LUCILLE ARP: Not to me it didn't. Looked like a

belly button to me. The inside part, way it folds over.

DORTIS MULKEY: You sure it was an ear? Sounds like it might have been something else.

LUCILLE ARP: That's what I thought. I saw that ear, I figured the mice must have eat up the rest, it was so old, and left the middle, where the hole is, and they puckered it up to sew it on.

DORTIS MULKEY: That right? Hell, that's nothing. I wouldn't go across the road to see it. Where else you been?

LUCILLE ARP: I been to Florida — *Suddenly remembering.* I been there two times.

DORTIS MULKEY: What's it like?

LUCILLE ARP: Rough. Florida was rough. It was the time before the land boom. We bought our first car and drove to Florida across the state line to Fernadina. It took us four days. Florida was rough.

DORTIS MULKEY: It ain't now — *suddenly excited.* It's smooth now. Slick as my palm, *and he lifts his right hand from the wheel to illustrate how slick his palm is.* That's where we'll go. I ain't never been there. O Lord, I always wanted to go to Florida, ain't you?

LUCILLE ARP: I been, and I found it rough. They got livestock on the beach.

DORTIS MULKEY: They ain't now. They cleaned it up, what I hear. Got more sights than you ever did see.

LUCILLE ARP: I seen it already. They got roaches big as birds.

156

DORTIS MULKEY: They fly?

LUCILLE ARP: Some of them do. Some of them crawl in the bed at night.

DORTIS MULKEY: That right? I wish I could see it.

LUCILLE ARP: You don't see it. You feel it. Feels like a cat under the covers.

DORTIS MULKEY: I don't mean roaches. I mean the whole place. I mean the whole state of Florida from top to bottom and side to side.

LUCILLE ARP: There's more top to bottom than there is side to side. That's in the section I taught on The Geography and Geology of Neighboring States. It ain't come out of the ocean long. Some parts still wet. Ain't run off yet.

DORTIS MULKEY: That's what I mean — *imagination working like a pump.* I told Sandy, I said, "I ain't staying here. Not when there's Florida I ant't never seen." And she said, "I can't leave my daddy."

LUCILLE ARP: Who's Sandy?

DORTIS MULKEY: Girl I'm fixing to marry. *Corrects himself:* I mean I might marry, when I retire from race car driving. I told you about that.

LUCILLE ARP: I remember. I was thinking about that, and I figure it's too dangerous. I might have to tell your momma.

DORTIS MULKEY: Go on and tell her, you know where she is. You know where she is, you know more than I do.

LUCILLE ARP: What happened? She run off?

DORTIS MULKEY: I don't know. I ain't never seen her. She was gone before my time. I ain't never missed her — *defensively. Then he falls silent.* I think she's in Tampa. Tampa, Florida. That's where they said she went. Said she couldn't stay at home. Said it was too sad.

LUCILLE ARP: What was too sad?

DORTIS MULKEY: Living with me. Said it was too rough. I made her tired.

LUCILLE ARP: You looking for your momma in Florida? That why you going?

DORTIS MULKEY: Hell no! I wouldn't even go to see her. I don't blame her. I'd have done the same thing myself if I was her and had to sit home and take care of me. But I wouldn't go nowhere to see her. If she was walking down the street going one way and I was going down the other, I'd cross over to the other side. She's dead to me. She died when she left.

LUCILLE ARP: I believe you. I feel the same way about Hollis, and he ain't even no kin to me. I wouldn't want to say hello if I had to. He was dead to me before I met him.

DORTIS MULKEY: Damn right. We ain't going to Tampa, are we? We're going to Miami. That's where we're going. We're going to Panama City, Boca Raton, Fort Myers, Key Largo —

LUCILLE ARP: Good old Rooster. *She reaches forward and touches his neck.* Your hair in the sun's like golden wire. Golden arms. You got golden arms... Driving your momma, going to Florida. We already on the way. I know that for certain. I know that the same way I know my own name.

DORTIS MULKEY: Yes Ma'am. You know what I feel like? I feel like a possum.

LUCILLE ARP: A possum?

DORTIS MULKEY: Yes Ma'am. One of them possums dead on the highway. Sandy says that's how they come.

LUCILLE ARP: What comes?

DORTIS MULKEY: Possums. Sandy says that's their natural state. You ever see one alive? She says that proves it. They're all born dead on the highway.

LUCILLE ARP: I don't believe that.

DORTIS MULKEY: Maybe not, but that's how I feel. I feel like I'm dead on the highway back yonder and just been born both at the same time.

LUCILLE ARP: What you mean?

DORTIS MULKEY: I got me a future, that's what I mean. I don't even know where I'm going, that's how free I am.

LUCILLE ARP: What?

DORTIS MULKEY: All that landscape flying past. That's what I call the future. You don't even know what it looks like till all of a sudden it's flying past and something else coming up. It's like you're getting born every minute.

LUCILLE ARP: Makes me dizzy, it's going so fast.

DORTIS MULKEY: You know what I feel like? I feel like a dog let out of a pen, don't you? I feel like a dog running around barking — *barks*.

Lucille Arp barks back. They laugh together.

DORTIS MULKEY: You ever been to Disney World?
— *turning back to see her in the dark.*

LUCILLE ARP: Where is that, in California?

DORTIS MULKEY: Orlando, Florida. You ain't never heard of Disney World? You ever hear of Walt Disney?

LUCILLE ARP: Of course I have, you ignorant boy.

DORTIS MULKEY: Well, he's the one made it. Just like the movies. *There is no answer from Lucille Arp. Dortis Mulkey checks it out in the rear view mirror. She is still sitting upright, hair sizzling in the light. He is afraid she might have died from excitement.* You park your car at one of the Dwarfs, Sleepy, or Sneezy — one of them in *Snow White* — and get in a train that goes through the gates. And you get inside, they got palaces. They got whole palaces made out of ice that never melts. And different lands.

LUCILLE ARP: Different lands.

DORTIS MULKEY: Yes Ma'am. That's what I hear. They got the Land of the Western Killers.

LUCILLE ARP: Western Killers.

DORTIS MULKEY: Yes Ma'am. Shoot you down in the streets at noon. And Energy Land and Space Exploration.

LUCILLE ARP: Space Exploration?

DORTIS MULKEY: Yes, Ma'am. Shoot you off in a rocket. And Undersea Land. Put you in a submarine under Lake Buena Vista. Goes on tracks. Plastic fish.

Moray eels got teeth in them. Chew on the sides. Chinese Ovaries.

LUCILLE ARP: Chinese Ovaries?

DORTIS MULKEY: Yes Ma'am. Four hundred brilliant birds flying from limb to limb. You ought to see it. You ain't never seen nothing like it, Sandy says. Sandy says she can have her a family and live in a trailer in back of her daddy the rest of her life now she's been there and seen all that. Nature in her Radiance. That's something else. World Village Craftsmen inlay gold in their hands. River Land. You ain't never seen nothing like it. *He gestures toward the windshield at the world fleeting past.* See that? That's ordinary. That's just the way it is. That ain't nothing. But Disney World — that's something else.

LUCILLE ARP: Well what we waiting for? Let's go. *She shouts so suddenly Dortis Mulkey does not know for a moment what she is talking about.*

DORTIS MULKEY: Go? Go where? You mean Disney World?

LUCILLE ARP: I mean Florida and all the rest. *She caresses his neck.* There's lots of things you ain't seen yet, Rooster. I'm going to take you. You still so young. You got the whole world laid out before you like some kind of music.

DORTIS MULKEY: You, too. Both together. You ain't been there either, have you?

LUCILLE ARP: That's why they put us in Hollis' car — *beating him on the shoulder.* That's the whole reason for it. Don't you see that, you ignorant boy? I see it clear now. The occult purpose. Look out there — *out the window.* I never knew the world was so lovely. I never knew I loved it so much.

DORTIS MULKEY: You hungry? You want you a Coca-Cola?

LUCILLE ARP: If I was thirsty I might. I never ate a Coca-Cola.

DORTIS MULKEY: What? What you mean eat it? You mean the bottle?

LUCILLE ARP: I mean you don't eat a Coca-Cola. Pay attention.

DORTIS MULKEY: What you do with it then — *still confused.*

LUCILLE ARP: You drink it, you ignorant boy.

DORTIS MULKEY: Peanuts then — *too happy to be put down.* Peanuts and Coca-Cola, how about that? Put them in and shake it up. Ever do that?

LUCILLE ARP: Of course I have. You think I was born yesterday?

DORTIS MULKEY: No Ma'am — *looking at her.* I know you wasn't.

LUCILLE ARP: Homer taught me. I poured in the peanuts, shook it up, and it exploded all over. *She looks out the window.* That's how I feel now — *suddenly.* I feel like I got peanuts in me. I'm about to pop.

DORTIS MULKEY: Me, too. That's how I feel ever since we got going to Disney World, ain't you? I'm about to pop. I thought to myself I feel like a Coca-Cola got peanuts in it somebody shook up. I'm about to pop. That's what made me think about it. That and I'm hungry. Ain't you?

Dortis Mulkey checks the rear view mirror searching for her face. And that's when he sees it: siren wailing, lollipop flashing — flat-round-flat-round — like a coin.

DORTIS MULKEY: Hold on. *He floorboards it almost by instinct. The car surges forward as though straining to catch up to itself. Lucille Arp is flung down into the back seat. It happens before she can even cry out or struggle against it until she finally pulls herself upright enough to beat on Dortis Mulkey's head and shoulders.*

LUCILLE ARP: Slow down, you damn fool. You'll kill us both.

DORTIS MULKEY: Look back — *trying to keep the car in control.*

LUCILLE ARP: What is it?

DORTIS MULKEY: State Patrol.

LUCILLE ARP: Who they after? Pull over. Let them pass. You're in the way.

DORTIS MULKEY: Us. They're after us.

LUCILLE ARP: What for?

DORTIS MULKEY: Hollis!

LUCILLE ARP: Drive on. Give him the slip. Don't stop now. There's Unadilla coming up. Turn off there, you hear me? Give him the slip.

DORTIS MULKEY: Yes Ma'am. *He leans right then left, then left again.*

LUCILLE ARP: You're doing fine. That's the way

Homer did it. Keep on going. It's right down here.

DORTIS MULKEY: I'm going.

LUCILLE ARP: What speed is it?

DORTIS MULKEY: Eighty-seven. *The State Patrol is still behind them. The wail of the siren is like a scream rising and falling.*

LUCILLE ARP: That's good. That's good. Eighty-seven. Go on up to ninety. I sure wish they'd turn that off, don't you.

DORTIS MULKEY: Yes Ma'am. We're coming in the main part of town.

LUCILLE ARP: Don't stop. Go on through. Don't stop for red lights. There's my house — *going past.*

DORTIS MULKEY: Yes Ma'am. Looks nice.

LUCILLE ARP: Don't stop now. Keep on to Florida.

The chase finally ends in a wreck. Noise. Smoke. Flashing lights.

DORTIS MULKEY, *shouting:* Look out. *He flings his arm out as though to catch Lucille Arp. His head ricochettes off the steering wheel a glancing blow and hits the dashboard. The skin on his forehead slits like a cloth split with a scissors. He falls on the floor under the wheel.*

A black patrolman rushes forward, drawing his pistol as he runs. He crouches in a firing position directly in front of the car, knees bent, steadying the pistol with both hands. He is aiming at the driver, to take him out. But Dortis Mulkey is still heaped on the floor under the dashboard. The pistol is pointed

*instead directly at Lucille Arp, who is sitting composed
on the back seat arranged as though for burial. Her
eyes are open like a camera fitted with a fisheye lens,
looking out in all directions at once, one hundred and
eighty degrees, seeing all the way to Florida. Her eyes
blaze with light.*

*The patrolman approaches the car cautiously. He
sees Dortis Mulkey, puts his revolver back in its
holster, and begins hauling him out, kicking the side of
the car for power. Dortis Mulkey tumbles out as
though fresh born, regaining consciousness just as he
falls. The patrolman grabs him by the collar and drags
him backwards toward the patrol car. Dortis Mulkey is
half leaning on the patrolman, half running, trying to
keep his feet under him.*

PATROLMAN: Your Momma's dead.

DORTIS MULKEY: What? My Momma? My
Momma's dead? *Crying out as he understands:*
Momma! Momma! *And again as he is pulled away
backwards:* Momma! Momma! It's Rooster!